When you have only two pennies
left in the world,
buy a loaf of bread with one,
and a lily with the other.

❦

CHINESE PROVERB

HOTPOTS:

Treasured Recipes from Friends of the Cincinnati Flower Show
©2003 Cincinnati Horticultural Society
All Rights Reserved.

Cookbook Committee	John Angelo	Marie Huenefeld
	Debbie Boehm	Kelly Mahan
	Nancy Brinker	Martha Seaman
	Jeane Elliott	Mona Wise
	Marsha Haberer	
	Barbara Hildebrandt	
Graphic Design	Susan M. Young	
Copyright Photo Acknowledgements	Paula Norton	

ISBN: 0-9740873-0-0

Proceeds from the sale of this book benefit ongoing programs of The Cincinnati Horticultural Society.
Additional copies: visit www.cincyflowershow.com.
Every effort has been made to give accurate and complete information throughout the book. We regret any errors or omissions.

Flower pot on opening page
Queen City Lace: SPONSOR: CINERGY FOUNDATION, ARTIST: BEV KIRK

▼ **Flower pots from left to right**
Snug as a Bud in a Rug: SPONSOR: GERALD & JAN BROWN CHECCO, ARTIST: JOANNE HONSCHOPP, *Chrysanthemummies*: SPONSOR: THE CROSSET FAMILY FUND, ARTIST: COOKI THIER, *I'm Stuck on Honey Suckle*: SPONSOR: DARLENE ANDERSON, ARTIST: KIRSTEN STAMATES, *Exposure to Beauty Breeds Beauty*: SPONSOR: THE CIVIC GARDEN CENTER OF CINCINNATI, ARTIST: FRAN KELLINGTON, *Birds of a Feather Flowered Together, Birds of a Feather Lost Forever*: SPONSOR: CINCINNATI MUSEUM CENTER, ARTIST: BURT DEVERE

ACKNOWLEDGEMENTS

Many friends assisted us when we
embarked on the project to produce
Hotpots, a cookbook in celebration of
fifteen years of the Flower Show. We hope you
will enjoy reading and using the recipes, based
on well-loved favorites, from people who have
given their support through the years.

We especially want to thank Jeane Elliott, CHS
Director of Marketing and Administration, and
Susan Young, freelance graphic designer, who
labored way above the call of duty to bring this
cookbook to fruition.

Thank you to all those who have helped us,
and we look forward to your help for the next
fifteen years.

Marsha Haberer
Chairman of the Board

Mary Margaret Rochford
President

TABLE OF CONTENTS

Coming Together for a Better Life
SPONSOR: PROCTER AND GAMBLE,
ARTIST: JIMI JONES

Worries go better

with soup

than without.

— YIDDISH PROVERB

SOUPS

Wild Rice Soup

Soups

2 cans ready-to-use chicken broth
1 can cream of celery soup
2 cups of water
1 box long-grain & wild rice mix (6 oz.)
2 cups cooked ham chunks
1 package frozen cut green beans (16 oz.)
1 tbsp. browning & seasoning sauce

Boil chicken broth, celery soup, water and rice mix. Reduce the heat to low, cover and simmer for 25 minutes. Return the heat to high, and stir in the ham, thawed green beans, and browning sauce. Cook for 5-8 minutes.

[My Cooking Tip]
"Take a deep breath, and clean up as you go along."
— *John*

Note: This is the perfect soup to make with leftovers. Any leftover holiday ham, turkey, chicken or beef can be cut into chunks and added to the soup. ❀

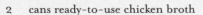

[On Gardening]
"Hire someone else to do it."
— *Cammy*

Flower Power
"It's groovy, baby!"
– Cammy

Patriotism in Bloom
SPONSOR: CLARK, SCHAEFER,
HACKETT & CO.,
ARTIST: COOKI THIER

End of the Rainbow ◭
SPONSOR: PNC BANK,
ARTIST: TONI PEDERSON, ARTISTS' ATTIC

Luck o' the Iris
SPONSOR: HOGAN FINANCIAL
SERVICES, INC.,
ARTIST: AMANDA HOGAN
CARLISLE

[JOHN'S WORDS OF WISDOM]
We WILL get through this!

Celebration of Life
SPONSOR: KRIS AND
CARL KALNOW,
ARTIST: LYNN KAHLE

ALBERTA MARSH
Community Volunteer

Buttermilk Soup with Cucumber and Crab

Soups

Low-fat buttermilk and nonfat yogurt
provide the base in a refreshing tangy soup.

3	large cucumbers
	(about 2 1/2 lbs.)
	peeled, seeded
1 cup	low-fat (1%) buttermilk
1/2 cup	plain nonfat yogurt
1/3 cup	chopped onion
1 1/4 tsp.	ground cumin
8 oz.	crabmeat, drained
1	ripe tomato, seeded, chopped
3	green onions, thinly sliced

[WORDS OF WISDOM]

*Organize your
clipped recipes.*

Chop 2 1/4 cucumbers; purée chopped
cucumbers, buttermilk, yogurt, onion
and cumin in blender until smooth.
Season with salt and pepper. Cover,
chill until very cold – at least 4 hours.
Can be made 1 day ahead and kept in
refrigerator.

Finely chop remaining 3/4 cucumber.
Mound crabmeat in center of 8 bowls,
dividing equally. Ladle cold soup
around crabmeat. Sprinkle with tomato,
green onions and finely chopped
cucumber.

Serves 8 ❋

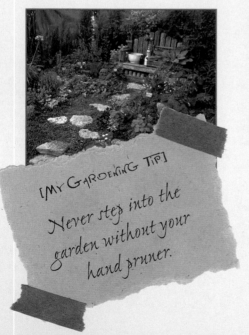

[MY GARDENING TIP]
*Never step into the
garden without your
hand pruner.*

Sales Manager, Comey & Shepherd/Flower Show Gala Co-Chair 2003

Chilled Strawberry Vodka Soup

3 pints	fresh or frozen strawberries
1/2 cup	sugar
1/2 cup	water
1/2 cup	or to taste vodka (unflavored)
1	fresh lemon
1 pint	Graeter's lemon sherbet fresh mint leaves

Purée strawberries in blender and strain with a sieve until all seeds are removed. Stir sugar into water until it is dissolved then add to strawberries. Add vodka and 2 tablespoons of lemon juice. Chill until very cold.

Serve in shallow crystal or white bowls, add 1 scoop Graeter's Lemon Sherbet to the center of each bowl, garnish with fresh mint and a thin lemon slice. Best in summer as a light dessert after fish or chicken.

I first tasted this soup in Cannes, France, in April 2000 on a family trip with my 83-year-old mother-in-law and other members of our extended family. I devised the recipe by sampling two bowls of it, by then, the proportions were irrelevant. I often add raspberries to change the flavor and the vodka proportions depending on the age of the crowd! ❀

[On Gardening]

I have a small herb garden outside my kitchen door. My favorites, which last almost all winter, are rosemary, sage, thyme and mint. Basil lasts for only two months in the garden in the summer, but still a favorite with tomatoes and fresh mozzarella. Even in January, I am still using rosemary and sage from the garden!

JEAN-ROBERT DE CAVEL
Chef/Owner, Jean-Robert at Pigall's

Late Summer Melon Gazpacho with Small Shrimp and Herb Salad

GAZPACHO:

1/4	cantaloupe melon
1/4	bulb of fennel
1	tomato
1/2	red, green and yellow pepper, seeded
1/4	stalk of celery branch
1/4	onion
6 oz.	watermelon, peeled, seeded
1/4	cucumber, peeled, seeded
3 slices	bread, no crust
1/4 tbsp.	Tabasco or as you wish for spice level
1 1/2 oz.	lemon juice
8 oz.	tomato juice
	salt and pepper to taste

Bon Appétit,
Jean-Robert

Mix everything together.
Marinate overnight for 24 hours.
Pass through a meat grinder or blender.
Salt and pepper to taste.

Serves 6 ❧

SHRIMP SALAD:

6 oz.	cooked small shrimp
1 sprig	basil
1 sprig	cilantro
1 sprig	mint
1 oz.	mayonnaise
3 tbsp.	ketchup
1 splash	brandy
2 oz.	cantaloupe melon
2 oz.	cucumber
2 oz.	watermelon

Blend mayonnaise, ketchup and brandy together. Chop cilantro, mint and basil. Cut melon, watermelon and cucumber into small dices. Mix dressing, melon, cucumber, herb and shrimp together. Salt and pepper to taste. Keep cold.

<u>Ready to Serve:</u>
Place gazpacho in a bowl. Add shrimp in the middle. Serve chilled. ❧

[MY WINE SUGGESTION]

Bandol
Rosé

JOHN CRANLEY
Cincinnati City Council

Spinach Tortellini Soup

Budding Young Artists
SPONSOR: KNOWLEDGEWORKS
FOUNDATION, ARTIST: 1ST GRADE
CLASS OF JULIE WITTEKIND AT ST.
CATHARINE OF SIENA

Dahlia Pot
SPONSOR: IN MEMORY OF
CAMILLA WARRICK,
ARTIST: M. KATHERINE
HURLEY

**Leadership
Zinnia-nati**
SPONSOR: LEADERSHIP
CINCINNATI ALUMNI,
ARTIST: JULIE RIEHLE

2 tbsp.	olive oil
4 oz.	ham diced (optional)
3	cloves minced garlic
1	med. onion, finely chopped
9 cups	chicken broth
2 tsp.	herb blend (Italian)
9 oz.	tortellini
1 can	crushed tomatoes, purée (28 oz.)
8 oz.	spinach-steamed and chopped
1 cup	Parmesan cheese
	salt and pepper to taste

Heat oil, add ham, garlic, onion and brown lightly – add broth and herbs. Boil and stir in tortellini, simmer uncovered until tortellini is cooked (12 min). Stir in tomato and simmer 5 min. Add spinach until wilted – season with salt and pepper – when in bowls top with Parmesan cheese.

For vegetarians the ham can be omitted, for vegans, omit ham and use vegetable broth and do not top with cheese. ❧

*Politicians can never have
enough ham.
– John*

JANET NEYRINCK
Personal Chef

Chicken Mulligatawny Soup

1	large onion diced
1	large garlic clove minced
1/2	large green bell pepper diced
1/2	large red bell pepper diced
2 tbsp.	ginger root minced
1/2 tbsp.	oil olive or canola
2 tbsp.	curry powder
1 tsp.	thyme, ground or fresh leaves if available
1 tbsp.	cumin seeds, ground
1	can diced tomatoes (15 oz.)
8 oz.	chicken, boneless cooked and shredded
3 cups	chicken broth
3/4 cup	rice
1/2 cup	heavy cream

A flavorful starter for an Indian inspired meal. Enjoy!
— Janet

Wash and cut the onions and peppers. Sauté the onion, garlic and peppers in 1/2 tablespoon of oil. Cook until wilted and opaque. Add the tomatoes and spices. Stir. Add the chicken broth and rice. Bring to a boil and cook until the rice is tender but not mushy. Add the chicken and stir to combine. Heat well. Add the heavy cream. Serve with a good hoppy beer such an IPA and bread or toasted pita.

Serves 6 ❧

PHILLIP LONG
Director, Taft Museum

Leopard Soup

1	package frozen peas
1	small onion, chopped
1	package frozen spinach
2 1/2 cups	chicken stock
1/4 tsp.	salt
	white pepper to taste
1 cup	half and half cream
1/2	bay leaf
1	sprig parsley
1/4 tsp.	chervil
1/4 tsp.	tarragon

Put the peas, onion, spinach and herbs in a saucepan with 1 cup of the chicken broth and simmer for 20-25 minutes. Purée in a blender and strain through a fine sieve. Add the cream and the remaining chicken broth. Add salt and pepper to taste. Chill until very cold.

Serves 8 ❋

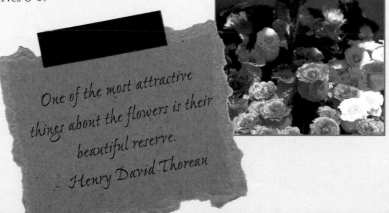

One of the most attractive things about the flowers is their beautiful reserve.

– Henry David Thoreau

HEATHER FRENCH HENRY

Miss America 2000/2000 Flower Show Honorary Guest

Lobster Bisque

2 tbsp.	oil
1 tbsp.	garlic
1 tbsp.	shallots
4	carrots
4	celery stalks (large)
1	onion (medium)
1	lobster cavity
1/2 tbsp.	peppercorns (whole)
3	bay leaves
1 tbsp.	thyme
1/2 oz.	lobster base
8 oz.	tomato purée
1 gallon	water
1/2 cup	sherry
1/2 cup	flour
1/2 cup	butter
1 tbsp.	butter
1 tbsp.	paprika
3 cups	heavy cream
4 oz.	lobster meat with juices
	salt and pepper to taste

My most favorite soup ...
Delicious! – Heather

Heat oil in pan. Chop garlic, shallots, carrots, celery, and onion. Sauté in hot oil until onion becomes transparent. Add bay leaves, thyme, peppercorns, and lobster cavity. Sauté all ingredients until the vegetables turn brown.

Use 1/3 cup of the sherry to deglaze the pan, then add tomato purée, lobster base, and water. Melt butter in a sauce pan, then add flour and blend with a wire whisk. Next add paprika, stirring vigorously with whisk. Set aside.

Let the stock reduce to 3/4 of a gallon, skimming top layer of oil off as it reduces. Next strain the stock through a fine sieve and reserve the liquid. Put the stock on heat and add your roux. After this you will strain through your sieve again. Add cream, lobster meat and juices, remaining sherry, and salt and pepper to taste.

From Historic Country Inns of Lexington, Virginia. ❈

HOPE TAFT
First Lady of Ohio

Gingered Carrot Soup with Roasted Pecans

3/4 cup	onions, chopped
2-3 tbsp.	fresh ginger, chopped
2 tbsp.	unsalted butter
4 cups	carrots, sliced thin
1/4 tsp.	ground cumin
1/2 tsp.	salt
3 cups	chicken stock
2 tbsp.	pecans, chopped
1 tsp.	butter
1/4 cup	fresh orange juice
1/4 cup	sour cream

Preheat oven to 350 degrees. In a saucepan cook onion and ginger in butter over moderate heat, stirring until softened. Add carrots, cumin, and salt and cook, stirring 1 minute. Add chicken stock and simmer mixture, covered, 25 minutes or until carrots are very tender. Prepare pecans while carrot soup is simmering: on a baking sheet toast pecans in middle of oven 8 minutes, or until fragrant and 1 shade darker. Toss pecans with butter and salt to taste. In a blender purée soup until smooth. Stir in the orange juice and correct the seasonings.

To serve; ladle soup into bowls, top with a teaspoonful of sour cream and the chopped pecans. ❀

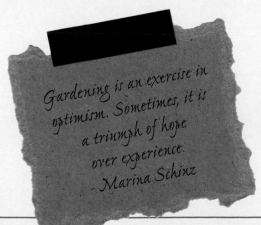

Gardening is an exercise in optimism. Sometimes, it is a triumph of hope over experience.
- Marina Schinz

PHYLLIS W. SMALE

CHS Founding Member

Leek, Potato and Sausage Soup

1/4 tsp.   cumin seeds
1/4 tsp.   caraway seeds
1 tbsp.   unsalted butter
1   medium leek-halved lengthwise,
           washed and green top trimmed off
2 cups   chicken broth
1   red potato, peeled and cubed
1/4 lb.   kielbasa, cut crosswise and
           sliced quartered
1 tbsp.   heavy cream (I leave this out)
1/4 cup   sliced spinach leaves (I use more)

In a dry, heavy pan, toast cumin seeds and caraway seeds over moderate heat. Remove to small dish. Slice the leeks thinly. Melt butter in pan and cook leeks until soft. Stir in broth and potato and bring to a boil. Simmer for five minutes. Return the seeds and add Kielbasa. Simmer five minutes, stir in cream and season with salt and pepper to taste. Add spinach and heat just until hot.

Serves 2 ❈

JOHN & PHYLLIS SMALE

*I often change recipe
for more portions and
increase spinach, kiel-
basa and potato.
        — Phyllis*

Shrimp Gazpacho Soup and Salad Combo

2 lbs.	fresh shrimp, peeled and deveined
4 cups	V-8 juice
2 cups	tomato juice
1 cup	Worcestershire sauce
2 tbsp.	Tabasco sauce
Splash	red wine vinegar
2 tsp.	sugar
	salt and pepper to taste
1-2 cups	salsa
1 cup	peeled, seeded, diced cucumber
1 cup	diced yellow tomatoes
1/4 cup	drained capers
4	avocados, peeled and diced

[On Gardening]

Remember to take time to stop and smell the roses.
— Debbie

Steam or sauté shrimp until pink; place in bowl and let cool. Combine V-8, tomato juice, Worcestershire, Tabasco, red wine vinegar, sugar, salt & pepper; pour over shrimp and marinate in refrigerator 2 hours. To serve, combine salsa, cucumber, tomatoes and capers. Layer avocado, salsa mix and shrimp (reserve marinade) evenly between 4 tall pilsners or wine goblets, alternating layers until glasses are filled. Pour in reserved marinade to fill.

Serves 4 ❀

Serve this flavorful & spicy "shrimp gazpacho" in tall pilsners or wine goblets for elegant & easy warm-weather entertaining — Debbie

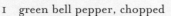

MARSHA HABERER
Chairman of the Board, The Cincinnati
Horticultural Society

Mexican Chicken Soup

1	green bell pepper, chopped
1	small onion, chopped
1 tbsp.	vegetable oil
2	cans chicken broth (32 oz. each)
1	can black beans, rinsed and drained (15 oz.)
1	can kidney beans, rinsed and drained (15 oz.)
1	can diced tomatoes (14 1/2 oz.)
3 cups	chopped cooked chicken
1 cup	frozen corn
1 tsp.	pepper
1/2 tsp.	salt
1/2 tsp.	ground cumin
2 tbsp.	chopped fresh cilantro
2 tbsp.	fresh lime juice

Garnishes: lime slices, tortilla chips,
sour cream, fresh cilantro

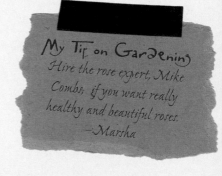

My Tip on Gardening
Hire the rose expert, Mike
Combs, if you want really
healthy and beautiful roses.
—Marsha

Sauté bell pepper and onion in hot oil
in a large Dutch oven over medium-
high heat for five minutes. Stir in
chicken broth and next 8 ingredients,
and bring to a boil. Reduce heat and
simmer, stirring occasionally 20 minutes.
Remove from heat, stir in cilantro and
lime juice. Garnish, if desired.

Makes 11 cups. ❀

Always think "color" when planning a meal. —Marsha

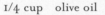

JIMMY GHERARDI
Chef, J's Seafood Restaurant

Spicy Conch Chowder

1/4 cup	olive oil
2 cups	chopped onions
1 cup	chopped red bell pepper
1/2 cup	chopped carrots
1/2 cup	chopped celery
3-4	cloves chopped garlic
1 lb.	ground conch
1/2 tsp.	dried oregano
1/2 tsp.	dried basil
1/2 tsp.	dried thyme
2	cans diced tomatoes (14 1/2 oz.)
2 cups	clam juice
1 cup	dry white wine
1	whole scotch bonnet pepper, or hot chili pepper
	salt and pepper to taste

Heat the olive oil in a large non-reactive stockpot over medium heat. Add the onions, red bell pepper, carrots, celery and garlic. Sauté until the vegetables are soft. Add the conch, oregano, basil, and thyme. Cook 4-5 minutes stirring often. Add the tomatoes, clam juice, wine, and the whole hot pepper. Bring to a boil. Reduce the heat to a simmer, season with salt and pepper and cook for about 40 minutes. ✽

*One cannot think well,
love well, sleep well, if one
has not dined well.
– Virginia Woolf*

LENORE AND DAVID NICHOLS

Friends of the Flower Show

Curried Lentil, Potato, and Spinach Soup

1 1/2 tbsp.	canola oil
1	large onion, chopped
8 cups	vegetable broth
1 cup	lentils, rinsed
1	large celery stalk, diced
4 cloves	garlic, minced
2	bay leaves
2	large all-purpose potatoes, scrubbed and diced
1	can diced tomatoes undrained (28 oz.)
2 tsp.	curry powder
1 tsp.	turmeric
1 1/2 tsp.	cumin
2	large carrots, sliced
1	package frozen chopped spinach, thawed and drained
2 tbsp.	fresh cilantro, chopped
1/2	lemon, juice of
1	dash salt
1	dash pepper

Heat the oil in a soup pot. Add the onion and sauté over moderately low heat until golden. Add the vegetable broth, lentils, celery, garlic, and bay leaves. Bring to a simmer, then simmer gently, covered for about 10 minutes.

Add the potatoes, carrots, tomatoes, turmeric, cumin and curry powder and simmer until the vegetables are tender, about 30 minutes. Stir in the spinach, cilantro, and lemon juice. Adjust the consistency with water if necessary, then season to taste with salt and pepper. Simmer over very low heat for another five minutes.

8 Servings ❀

JAN LAINE
Flower Show Volunteer

Gazpacho I

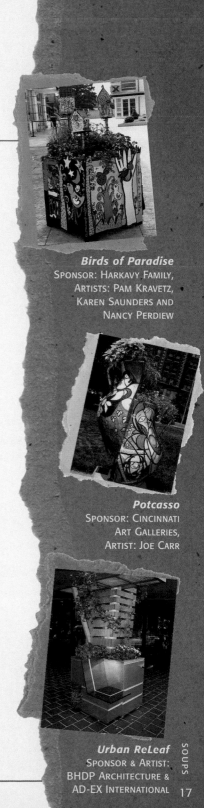

1 peeled and seeded cucumber
   parsley
1 seeded green pepper
1 medium onion

Place veggies in food processor and chop. Add 1 –
8oz. bottle Kraft Catalina dressing, 1 large can of
tomato juice (48 oz.) and mix. Serve well chilled. Is
very good served hot also.

Serves 6-8 ❋

We used to serve this as a tradition at the
Civic Garden Center Plant and Herb Sale
Lunches. It was heated and served hot on
some of the cooler May days.
– Jan

Birds of Paradise
SPONSOR: HARKAVY FAMILY,
ARTISTS: PAM KRAVETZ,
KAREN SAUNDERS AND
NANCY PERDIEW

Potcasso
SPONSOR: CINCINNATI
ART GALLERIES,
ARTIST: JOE CARR

Urban ReLeaf
SPONSOR & ARTIST:
BHDP ARCHITECTURE &
AD-EX INTERNATIONAL

SOUPS

17

Gazpacho II

Soups

1	clove garlic (finely chopped or run through a garlic press)
2 tbsp.	extra virgin olive oil
1 cup	finely chopped, seeded, peeled tomato
1/4 cup	finely chopped onion
1/2 cup	finely chopped green pepper
1/2 cup	finely chopped, seeded and peeled cucumber
1/2 cup	finely chopped celery

Vegetables can be chopped in a food processor, but hand chopped gives the best result.

3 tbsp.	tarragon vinegar (or 3 tablespoons champagne or white wine vinegar and a pinch of dried tarragon)
1 tsp.	salt (or less to taste)
1/4 tsp.	black pepper
1/2 tsp.	Worcestershire (eliminate if you want a completely vegetarian soup)
2 cups	tomato juice
2 tsp.	chopped parsley
1 tbsp.	snipped fresh chives or 1/3 teaspoon dried chives

Combine, cover and chill for a least three hours. Adjust thickness with V-8 or tomato juice as needed.

Serves 6 ❀

◀ *Flower Children*
SPONSOR: ZARING FAMILY FOUNDATION,
ARTIST: DAWNA BOEHMER

Really Red Soup

2 tbsp.	light oil (sesame/ safflower/peanut)
I	medium Vadalia (sweet) onion, chopped
2	large garlic cloves, crushed
8	plum or garden-ripe tomatoes
4	red bell peppers, roasted, peeled and quartered
I cup	chicken stock
1/2 cup	double cream, slightly warmed
	salt and pepper, freshly ground
4 tbsp.	fresh basil

As a winter substitute, add one 28 ounce can plum tomatoes.

In heavy saucepan, sauté onion and garlic in the oil until soft, about five minutes. Add peppers, tomatoes with juice and chicken stock. Cook on low heat 30 minutes. Strain out solids and purée in processor. Return all to liquid in pan and add the cream. Season to taste and add basil.

May be served hot or cold.

Serves 6 ✻

My kitchen is my refuge, and cooking is the best change-of-pace from the daily meetings. It is here that I become a free spirit.

— Joyce

JEROME (JERRY) EICHERT
CHS Treasurer and Volunteer Extraordinaire

Soup of the Bakony Outlaws

3 tbsp.	oil
2	onions, cut into 1/4-inch dice
2 oz.	bacon, cut into 1/4-inch dice
1 1/2 tbsp.	sweet Hungarian paprika
8 oz.	thin veal cutlet, cut into 1/4-inch dice
2 or 3 cups	homemade or low-salt canned chicken stock
2	medium carrots, cut into 1/4-inch dice
2	medium turnips, cut into 1/4-inch dice
8 oz.	mushrooms, cut into 1/4-inch dice
2	medium potatoes, cut into 1/4-inch dice
2	medium tomatoes, peeled, seeded & cut into 1/4-inch dice or 4 canned seeded, chopped tomatoes
	salt & freshly-ground black pepper
1 cup	sour cream
2 tbsp.	all-purpose flour
1 cup	heavy cream or crème fraîche
3 tbsp.	snipped fresh dill, plus sprigs for decoration

Bakony is a mountainous region near Lake Balaton in Hungary, about forty miles from Budapest. (According to an old legend, deep in the middle of Lake Balaton, there is a church with a girl inside, who is feeding the silky waters of the lake with her tears.) The Bakony outlaws must have been both gourmet and gourmand to inspire this hearty, flavorful soup. Mushrooms, which are an ingredient of the soup, seem to be a must in most other Bakony recipes; perhaps the outlaws were mushroom thieves. Notice that many of the ingredients are diced pretty finely, which gives the soup a wonderful texture and lots of flavor. If, however, you need to save some time you can chop a bit more coarsely. Be sure, though, to dice the bacon and veal very small.

Heat the oil in a large saucepan or Dutch oven and cook the onions and bacon over medium heat until the onions start to color (10 to 15 minutes). Stir in the paprika and cook, stirring, another 2 minutes to release and develop its flavor. Add the veal and just enough stock to cover it. Cover the pan and simmer for 20 minutes. Add the carrots, turnips, mushrooms, potatoes, tomatoes, and more stock, reserving about 1 cup of stock; don't worry if the liquid doesn't cover the vegetables at this point. Season with salt and pepper.

Bring to a boil, reduce the heat, and simmer until the vegetables are tender (another 20 minutes). Add a little more stock if the soup looks too dry during cooking, bearing in mind that more liquid will be added later. Put the sour cream in a small bowl and stir in the flour with a fork or whisk; stir in the cream. Pour this into the soup and bring to a boil, stirring constantly. Simmer for 2 minutes. Taste and adjust the salt and pepper. Just before serving, stir in the chopped fresh dill and toss some sprigs on top for decoration, if you like.

(Original recipe from The Taunton Store & Fine Cooking magazine)

Serves 4 as a meal or 8 as a first course. ❈

What Lies Beneath
SPONSOR: MILLER GALLERY FOR INDIAN HILL MIDDLE SCHOOL, ARTISTS: INDIAN HILL MIDDLE SCHOOL STUDENTS

Plant-it Ross
SPONSOR: ROSS HIGH SCHOOL, ARTIST: ROSS HIGH SCHOOL STUDENTS

Bigonia Boy
SPONSOR: FRISCH'S RESTAURANTS, INC., ARTIST: HOANG PHAM, ARTISTS' ATTIC

SOUPS

21

JAN KIVORA

Flower Show Volunteer and Exhibitor

Potato-Leek Soup

1/4 lb.	slab bacon, cut in 1/4 inch cubes
3	leeks, white part only, sliced 1/4 inch thick
1 cup	chopped celery with leaves
1/2 cup	chopped onion (I prefer sweet ones, like Vidalia)
2 cups	chicken broth
2-3	large russet potatoes, peeled and cut in 1/2 inch cubes
1/4 cup	chopped parsley (mostly leaves)
1/4 cup	all-purpose flour
2 cups	whole milk
1/4 tsp.	salt
1/4 tsp.	white pepper
1/8 tsp.	ground nutmeg
	butter to taste

In a 5-quart Dutch oven, over medium-high heat, brown bacon lightly. Remove bacon and set aside. Add leeks, celery, and onion to bacon drippings. Sauté for 10 minutes or until golden. Add broth and bacon. Reduce heat to low, cover and simmer for 15 minutes. Add potatoes and parsley and simmer for 20 minutes or until potatoes are tender. Beat flour into milk with a whisk (until smooth) and stir into soup mixture. Add salt, pepper and nutmeg. Stirring over medium heat, bring to a boil and cook for 2 minutes.

Ladle into bowls and top each serving with a pat of butter or shredded cheddar. Delicious with crusty bread!

Makes 4 servings. ✽

▲ JERRY JASPERS & JAN

One of my favorite garden tricks is for stabilizing heavy peonie stems. As you well know, your beautiful blossoms can often fall prey to the spring rains that weigh the blossoms down to the ground. Early in the season, I cut a good sized square of chicken wire and lay it over the new sprouts of the plant. As the sprouts grow, they take the mesh up with them, thus creating a very sturdy support system that is virtually invisible as the leaves fill in.

Tatonka Soup

1	medium onion, diced
1	leek, cut into rounds
4	ribs (stalks) celery, diced
2	medium carrots, diced
1/4 cup	green bell peppers, diced
1/4 cup	red bell peppers, diced
1/4 cup	oil
1 lb.	ground bison
2 tsp.	garlic, chopped
1/2 cup	tomato paste
1 1/2 qt.	bison stock
1 qt.	chicken stock
1 tsp.	black pepper, coarsely ground
1	bay leaf
1/2 tsp.	thyme leaves
1/2 tsp.	marjoram leaves
2 cups	red potatoes, peeled and cubed
2 cups	tomatoes, diced
1/2 cup	green beans, frozen
1/2 cup	corn, frozen

The Gift of Flowers of Hope From the King
SPONSOR: VOLUNTEERS OF THE CINCINNATI ART MUSEUM,
ARTIST: BRIAN JOINER

Sauté first six items in oil until onions are slightly browned. Add ground bison and cook it until meat is cooked to your satisfaction. Add the garlic, tomato paste, bison stock and chicken stock and the spices. Bring to a boil. Add the potatoes and diced tomatoes and simmer for 25 minutes. Add the green beans and corn. Cook for another 15-20 minutes.

Makes approximately 1 1/4 gallons. ❀

RUTH ROGERS CLAUSEN
Horticulture Editor
Country Living Gardener Magazine

Spinach and Watercress Soup

1	medium onion
2	carrots
4 cups	low-sodium chicken broth
1/2 tsp.	nutmeg
1 tsp.	salt, or to taste
1/2 tsp.	pepper
6 tbsp.	unsalted butter or olive oil
6 tbsp.	flour
3 cups	milk (can be 2%)
1/2 bunch	fresh spinach
1/2 bunch	fresh watercress
	zest of one lemon

[MY GARDENING TIP]

Remember that gardening is a way of life, not an activity to be completed as easily and rapidly as possible (except when it's "open garden tomorrow").

Chop the onion and carrots till fine in a food processor. Add to the broth along with seasonings and bring to a gentle boil. Simmer for 10 – 15 minutes.

Melt 6 tablespoons unsalted butter (or use 6 tablespoons olive oil) and make a roux with 6 tablespoons flour. Whisk in 1 cup of milk. (I use 2 %). Gradually stir into the broth mixture.

Wash and trim a half bunch of fresh spinach and a half bunch fresh watercress. Remove any tough stems; slice into thin ribbons, and add to the hot broth. Add the grated zest of one lemon and two cups more milk. (To make a very rich soup, you can use heavy cream, but milk tastes just fine). Serve hot or at room temperature.

Garnish with a fresh pesticide-free Johnny-Jump-Up blossom, Calendula petals, or chopped toasted nuts.

Makes about 8 cups. ❁

[On Flower Power]

"A wonderful idea continuing the work of turning Cincinnati into a garden city."

– Ruth

JOAN CROWE
Community Volunteer

Chunky Potato Cheddar Soup

3	medium red potatoes
2 cups	water
1	small onion
3 tbsp.	butter
3 tbsp.	flour
3 cups	milk
1 tsp.	sugar
1 cup	shredded cheddar cheese
1 cup	chopped cooked bacon

Peel potatoes and cut into 1-inch chunks. Bring 2 cups water to boil and add potatoes cooking until tender. Drain and reserve liquid. Measure 1 cup reserved liquid and set aside. Melt butter in pan. Peel and chop onion, and sauté until tender but not brown. Add flour to saucepan, season with salt and pepper. Cook three to four minutes. Add potatoes and reserved liquid, milk, sugar, onion mixture. Stir, add cheese and bacon. Simmer 30 minutes. 🌸

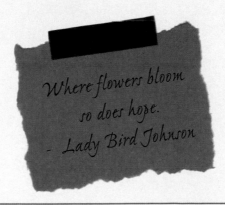

Where flowers bloom so does hope.
- Lady Bird Johnson

PAULA COMISAR
2003 Flower Show Gala Co-Chair

Italian Soup

2 lbs.	hot or mild sausage
3	carrots, chopped
1	onion, chopped
	some garlic chopped
3 quarts	chicken broth
2	cans diced tomatoes
2 cups	pasta of your choice
1	box of frozen spinach
	or 1 bunch fresh
	salt and pepper to taste

Squeeze sausage from casings, and cook until brown. Add carrots, onion and garlic, cooking until soft. Add broth, tomatoes in their juice, bringing to a boil. Add pasta, reduce heat, simmer covered until pasta is tender. Stir in spinach.

Voila!!!! ❀

*Let the stoics say what they please,
we do not eat for the good of living,
but because the meat is savory and
the appetite is keen.
- Ralph Waldo Emerson*

LEE CARTER
Chairman of the Board,
Cincinnati Children's Hospital Medical Center

Cold Tomato Soup

1 can	undiluted tomato soup
1 can	beef bouillon
8 oz.	sour cream
2 tbsp.	chopped green onion
1 tbsp.	red wine
1/2 tsp.	salt
1 tbsp.	fresh basil leaves

Mix all ingredients in a blender. Chill well. Best made the day before.

Serves 4-6 ❋

All Seasonsgood Pavillion
SPONSOR: GORDON AND
NADINE BRUNNER,
ARTIST: JoANN HEURICH

Pot Porri
SPONSOR: MARSHA AND
ED HABERER, ARTIST:
COLLEEN DOOLEY

▲ LEE, AT LEFT, WITH JIM ANDERSON
AND MARSHA HABERER

Age of Asparagus
SPONSOR: THE ALLEEN
COMPANY, ARTIST:
COOKI THIER

VICTORIA MORGAN
Artistic Director, Cincinnati Ballet

White Beans and Escarole Soup

2 tbsp.	olive oil
1	small onion
2 (+)	cloves of garlic, chopped finely
1	head of escarole, cored and finely chopped
1 - 16 oz.	can of peeled tomatoes
1/2 cup	water
1 can	cannellini beans, drained and rinsed (15 oz.)
1 cup	freshly grated Parmesan

(Recently discovered in New York Times Magazine)

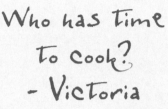

Who has time to cook?
- Victoria

Sauté onion and garlic in olive oil until softened. Add escarole and mix in; then add tomatoes and water and cook briefly. Add beans and heat through before finishing with Parmesan. ✳

RITA NADER HEIKENFELD
Culinary Expert

Rita's Light and Lively Chicken Gumbo

1-1/2 lbs.	boneless, skinless chicken breast cut into 1" pieces
	olive oil
1	bell pepper, diced
1	generous cup onion, diced
2	ribs celery, diced
1 tsp.	garlic, minced
1	bay leaf
4	cans good quality chicken broth or homemade stock (14 oz., approx. ea. can)
1 cup	rice
1 can	diced tomatoes (approximately 14 oz.)
1 tbsp.	fresh basil, chopped or 1 teaspoon dry
1 box	frozen cut okra thawed (10 oz.), or
2 cups	fresh okra, sliced

▲

Seasons Change
SPONSOR: TOWER PLACE AT THE CAREW TOWER, ARTIST: AMANDA BUTLER KOLAR

Have chicken at room temperature (bring out of refrigerator about 20 minutes prior to cooking). In large stockpot, add a bit of olive oil. Add chicken, bell pepper, onion, celery, garlic and bay leaf. Cook until chicken is almost done and vegetables smell aromatic, about 10 minutes. Add broth, rice and tomatoes. Bring to a boil. Lower to a simmer and cover. Cook at a gentle boil until rice is almost done, about 10-15 minutes. Add basil. Cook a few minutes more. While soup is cooking, sauté okra in a bit of olive oil just until crisp/tender and still bright green. Taste for salt and pepper. Add okra and serve.

Serves 12-15 ❀

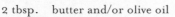

JON BRANSTRATOR
Chef's Collaborative

Corn and Green Chile Chowder

2 tbsp.	butter and/or olive oil
1	medium yellow onion
2	carrots diced
2	red bell peppers
3	roasted green chilies (roast over burner or on a gas grill, peel off charred skin)
2	jalapenos
4	medium red potatoes, peeled and cut in 3/4" dice
3 cups	chicken stock
2 cups	milk
1 tbsp.	cumin
6	ears of fresh corn or 4 cups corn kernels
1/4 cup	cilantro, chopped (stems & leaves)

Heat oil/butter in a 4-6 quart pot, add carrots and onion and sauté on low heat for 5 minutes without browning. Stir in red pepper and sauté for 3 more minutes. Add the cumin, jalapenos, green chilies, potatoes, milk, stock. Cover and simmer for about 20 minutes until the potatoes are tender. Use a potato masher to crush about 1/3 of the vegetables, add the corn and simmer for about 5 minutes.

Garnish each bowl with cilantro. ✿

While I was living in Prescott, Arizona, a local favorite was this corn and green chile chowder that was called Sonoran (the Mexican state south of Arizona.)

BUTCH CALLERY
Mayor, City of Covington

Callery Chili

1 lb.	ground beef
1	medium onion
1 tsp.	garlic salt
1 tsp.	salt
1 tbsp.	chili powder
1/2 tsp.	pepper
1 tsp.	cumin
1 tbsp.	packed brown sugar
1 lb.	can kidney beans
1 lb.	can tomatoes
1 lb.	can tomato sauce
1 tsp.	dried oregano

Cook meat and onion until meat is no longer pink. Add remainder of ingredients. Simmer 30 minutes, uncovered. ❀

Show Me the Monet
SPONSOR: CINCINNATI TOWN AND COUNTRY GARDEN CLUB, ARTIST: M. KATHERINE HURLEY

Flower Girls
SPONSOR: CINCINNATI FLOWER SHOW, ARTIST: JANICE AND RANDY CAMPION

▲ MAYOR CALLERY WITH MARY MARGARET ROCHFORD

A quick and easy chili recipe for busy politicians and everyone else who never have enough time to spend in the kitchen. – Butch

Beatrix Potter
SPONSOR: MATHIS FOUNDATION FOR CHILDREN, ARTIST: AMANDA HOGAN

SOUPS

31

DARINA ALLEN
Ireland's Ballymaloe Cookery School Proprietor
and 1999 Fall Flower & Farm Fest Guest Chef

White Winter Vegetable Soup

2 ozs.	(55 g/1/2 stick) butter
4 ozs.	(110 g/1 cup) onions
5 ozs.	(140 g/1 cup) potatoes
5 ozs.	(140 g/1 cup) white turnips, cut into 1/4 inch dice
4 ozs.	(110 g/1 cup) celery, cut into 1/4 inch dice
4 ozs.	(110 g/1 cup) parsnips, cut into 1/4 inch dice
4 ozs.	(110 g/1 cup) white part of leeks, cut into 1/4 inch dice
5 ozs.	(110 g/1 cup) cauliflower, cut into 1/4 inch dice
3 pints	(1.7 L/7 1/2 cups) home-made chicken stock
6-8 fl. ozs.	(175 –225 g/3/4 to 1 cup) creamy milk
	salt and freshly-ground pepper

Garnish with finely-chopped chives and croûtons.

Recipe with thanks to Gill and Macmillan, Ltd. Publisher

◀ ***A Cow Slips Through the Rookwoods***
SPONSOR: HELEN B. VOGEL TRUST, ARTIST:
SARAH VAUGHAN MURPHREE

Prepare all the vegetables. Melt the butter in a heavy saucepan; when it foams, add the potatoes and onions and toss until well coated with butter. Cover with a paper lid (to keep in the steam) and the saucepan lid. Sweat for 5 minutes approx. on a gentle heat, then add in the other diced vegetables. Season with salt and freshly ground pepper, cover and sweat for a further 5 minutes. Discard the paper lid. Add the stock; bring it to the boil until the vegetables are soft, 8-10 minutes approx. Liquidise the soup, taste and thin with creamy milk if necessary. Serve in soup bowls or in a soup tureen garnished with a blob of whipped cream, and sprinkle with a few finely-chopped chives.

Serves 8-9

CROÛTONS:

1 slice	slightly stale pan bread, 1/4 inch thick
1/2 oz.	(15 g) butter
1 tbsp.	(3 American tsp.) olive oil

First cut the crusts off the bread, next cut into 1/4 inch strips and then into exact cubes (a cube is a six-sided square with equal sides).

Melt the butter in a clean frying pan with the olive oil. Turn up the heat and add the croûtons. The pan should be quite hot at first, then reduce the heat to medium and keep tossing all the time until the croutons are golden brown all over. Drain on kitchen paper.

Serves 4. ❀

ROBERT LEE
Designer, Belle Maison

Pasta e Fagioli

16 oz.	jar Great Northern Beans, not drained
2 tbsp.	unsalted butter
2-3 ribs	celery chopped into small dice
1 medium	onion, finely chopped
2 tsp.	minced garlic
2 tbsp.	finely chopped rosemary
4 cups	chicken stock
1	medium Yukon gold potato
2	cans diced tomatoes
1 tsp.	salt
1/2 tsp.	freshly ground pepper
1/4 tsp.	Tabasco sauce
6 ozs.	farfalle pasta
1/4 cup	packed fresh basil leaves
1/4 cup	packed fresh parsley leaves
5	large fresh sage leaves
6 tbsp.	freshly grated Parmesan cheese

This traditional and healthful Italian soup is hearty enough to serve as a main course but can function well as a first course with a lighter entrée. Although fine when reheated, unlike many other soups, it is really best the first time. This is because the fresh herbs, both aromatic and flavorful are added at the end and because the pasta is cooked separately to just the right tenderness before adding the soup. It will not be the same or taste as good using dried herbs.

Melt butter in large enameled pan or stock pot. Add celery, onion and 1 1/2 teaspoons of garlic. Cook over medium heat until softened and translucent, about 5-6 minutes. Add the beans, 1 tablespoon rosemary, stock, potato, tomatoes, pepper, salt, Tabasco and 3 cups water. Combine well and lower heat to a simmer. Cook for about a half hour.

Cook pasta until al dente and set aside.

Remove about a third of the soup and purée in a processor. Return processed soup to stock pot and stir. Add pasta and keep warm on low heat.

Chop remaining garlic and rosemary, with basil, parsley and sage until finely minced. Stir into soup and ladle into bowls. Sprinkle each bowl with Parmesan and serve immediately. ❧

JEANE ELLIOTT
CHS Marketing and Administration Director

Cold Cucumber Soup

2 tbsp.	butter or margarine
1/2 cup	chopped green onion
2 cups	peeled and diced cucumber
1 cup	watercress or spinach
1/2 cup	raw, peeled, diced potato
2 cups	chicken broth
3/4 tsp.	salt
1/2 tsp.	white pepper
1 cup	heavy cream

Melt butter and cook onion on medium heat—5 minutes. Do not brown. Add cucumber, watercress, potato, broth, salt and pepper. Bring to boil and cook over low heat 15 minutes.

Purée in blender when slightly cool. Stir in cream and refrigerate several hours or overnight. Serve with chopped chives or cucumbers.

Serves 4-6. ❀

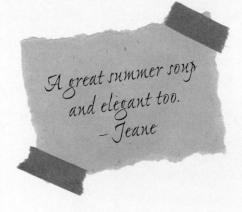

A great summer soup and elegant too.
— Jeane

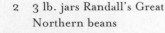

PAULA NORTON

Official Photographer of the Cincinnati Flower Show

White Chili Soup

SOUPS

2	3 lb. jars Randall's Great Northern beans
6 cups	chicken broth
2	cloves garlic, minced
1 tbsp.	oil
2	4 oz. cans chopped mild green chilies
2 tsp.	ground cumin
1 1/2 tsp.	oregano
1/4 tsp.	ground cloves
1/4 tsp.	cayenne pepper
8	pieces diced cooked chicken breasts
1	bottle of mild salsa
1	container sour cream
1	large chopped onion

Great when you want something a little different than regular chili.
– Paula

Cook eight chicken breast pieces in enough water to cover. Bring to a boil. This can be cooked the night before and chicken kept in refrigerator. Save broth.

Combine beans, broth, garlic and half the onions in a large soup pot. Bring to a boil, adding more broth if necessary.

In a skillet, sauté remaining onions in oil until tender. Add chilies, and seasonings and mix thoroughly. Add to bean mixture. Add chicken and simmer one hour.

Serve topped with salsa and sour cream.

Serves 10 ❁

DONNA WYMORE
Flower Show Volunteer

New Orleans Corn Bisque with Sausage

▲ DONNA AND DON WYMORE

4 tbsp.	butter or margarine
2 tbsp.	flour
1/2 cup	onion, chopped
1 pkg.	(1 lb) smoked sausage, cut into 1/4-inch slices
1 qt.	milk
1	can cream style corn (16 oz.)
1	can cream of potato soup, undiluted (10 1/2 oz.)
1 tbsp.	Tabasco® brand pepper sauce
1 tbsp.	cajun seasoning
1/2 cup	cheddar cheese, grated (optional)
1/4 cup	parsley, chopped (optional)

Melt butter, add flour; blend thoroughly then add onion and Hillshire Farm® Smoked Sausage. Sauté over medium heat for 5 minutes. Add next 5 ingredients (through Cajun seasoning), cover, and cook over low heat for 20 minutes. Stir occasionally. Just before serving, sprinkle with cheese and parsley, if desired. Yield: 2-1/2 qt.

Serves 8 ❋

Nothing takes the chill off a cool fall night better than a delicious bowl of soup. I guarantee this fuss-free soup is one you'll want to serve often! – Donna

SHARON HOVERSON
Flower Show Volunteer

Sausage and White Bean Soup

2 cups	dried white (navy) beans
8 cups	chicken stock
1/4 tsp.	dried thyme
1/4 cup	olive oil
1 1/2 cups	coarsely chopped onion
1/2 cup	coarsely chopped celery
2	large carrots, peeled and cut into rings
1/4	large green bell pepper, coarsely chopped
1	sausage (1 1/4 lbs.)
2	large garlic cloves, minced
1/4 cup	dry red wine

Pick over beans and soak overnight. Drain and place beans, chicken stock and thyme in a large pot. Bring to a simmer and continue to cook, skimming as necessary, until beans begin to get tender and fall apart, 1 1/2 – 2 hours. Add another 2 cups of chicken stock, or to taste, if soup has reduced too much at the end of the cooking time.

Meanwhile, place olive oil in a large skillet and sauté all the vegetables except the garlic until they start to brown. Scrape into a food processor and purée. Reserve this purée and add to the beans for the last 30 minutes of their cooking time.

Place sausage in a cold skillet and cook over high heat 6 minutes, turning often. Pour off the fat. Add the garlic and red wine. Simmer, covered, for another 15 minutes. Cut the sausages into rings and add to the soup. Degrease the pan with a few tablespoons of water or chicken stock, and then add to soup.

Recipe from "Lee Bailey's Soup Meals". ❧

Note from Lee
Make the soup a day or so in advance to allow flavors to meld. The sausages can also be cooked ahead, but don't mix them in until the soup is reheated prior to serving. (Stir the wine-garlic-sausage cooking liquid in the soup while the liquid is hot.)

You can use any sausage that appeals to you for this, but Polish sausage was used in the soups previously made. This method of cooking sausage is a good one; it's foolproof, and always improves the flavor of whatever sausage you are preparing.
– Sharon

CAROLE PHILIPPS
Writer and Former Editor of Cincinnati Post's At Home

Spiced Ham & Beans

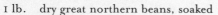

SOUPS

1 lb.	dry great northern beans, soaked	12	juniper berries
2	large onions, chopped	4	bay leaves
4	garlic cloves, peeled and sliced		water to cover (about
6 tbsp.	olive oil		8 cups)
1	bone from cooked ham with clinging bits of meat	1/2 lb.	diced or chopped cut up ham
16	dried peppercorns	1	can black beans (15-oz.),
16	dried allspice berries		drained and rinsed
			salt and pepper to taste

The evening before preparing soup, pick through beans, discarding any that are discolored. Soak beans overnight in 8 cups of cold water. Drain and discard soaking water before cooking.

The next day, heat olive oil in a large pot (big enough to hold the beans and the ham bone with room to spare). Sauté the onion and garlic in the oil until the onion grows clear, about 5 minutes.

Add the ham bone, beans and water to cover. Tie peppercorns, allspice berries, juniper berries and bay leaves loosely in cheesecloth and toss into the pot. Bring to boil then reduce to a slow simmer. Partially cover pot and cook over low heat for two hours, stirring occasionally and adding additional water if needed.

Take the pot from the stove. Remove the ham bone and set aside to cool. Add the rinsed black beans and the ham pieces to the pot. Return the beans to the stove and continue cooking very slowly with lid ajar for up to two hours. Stir regularly and keep heat low to prevent scorching and sticking. Add water only in small amounts if necessary. When ham bone is cool enough to handle, pick off any clinging meat and add to the pot.

When the beans reach a creamy consistency, remove from heat and allow to sit until fat rises. Skim and discard fat and discard the bag of seasonings. Add salt and pepper to taste and reheat gently before serving.

Variation: If you wish to avoid soaking the dry beans, the soup can be made with 1 quart (4 cups) of canned great northern beans. Rinse and drain the beans and reduce initial cooking time to 1 hour. Then add two cans of black beans, drained and rinsed, instead of one and continue with recipe.

A version of this appeared in the February 5, 1997, edition of "The Cincinnati Post".

Serves 4-6 ❋

LIZ BONIS
MIX 94.1 Morning Show Host

Pasta e Fagioli

2 tsp.	olive oil
1	small onion
2	cloves garlic, minced
2	cans reduced sodium, fat free chicken broth (14 1/2 oz. each)
1 can	diced tomatoes (15 oz.)
1 can	cannellini or white beans (15 oz.), rinsed and drained
1/2 cup	ditalini or other small pasta
1/2 lb.	Swiss chard or spinach leaves, coarsely chopped
1/4 tsp.	salt
	Parmesan cheese

Warm the oil in a large saucepan over medium heat. Add the onion and garlic. Cook, stirring occasionally, 3-5 minutes, or until the onion is soft.

Add the broth, tomatoes (with juice), beans and pasta. Cook, stirring occasionally for 15 minutes, or until the pasta is cooked. Add the swiss chard and salt. Cook, stirring occasionally, for 2-3 minutes longer or until the swiss chard is wilted. For added flavor, sprinkle grated Parmesan cheese and black pepper on the pasta e fagiole just before serving.

Recipe from "Prevention Magazine" — May 2003

Serves 6 ✽

There are no good or bad foods, only good or bad quantities of food.
— Liz

MICHAEL FISHER

President, Greater Cincinnati Chamber of Commerce

Cuban Black Bean Soup

1 lb.	dried black beans
8 cups	water
1/2	green pepper
1	large chopped onion
1/2	green pepper, diced
1-2	garlic cloves, diced
	oregano
2	bay leaves
	salt and pepper
2 tbsp.	apple vinegar
2 tbsp.	white cooking wine
1/2 tsp.	sugar

Put beans, water and green pepper in a pot overnight. The following day, put pot of beans to boil and then simmer for one hour.

Sauté onion, green pepper, garlic, oregano and bay leaves until vegetables are tender while listening to Buena Vista Social Club. Take 1/2 a ladle of black beans and slightly mash them into sauté onion mixture. Make sure you keep moving to the rhythm!

Put sauté mixture into pot of simmering black beans. Add apple vinegar. After 1/2 an hour add cooking wine and sugar. After simmering for another 1/2 hour taste for salt & pepper.

If you want to serve it as soup, you may want to add more water.

Courtesy of Michael Fisher's Cuban In-Laws. ✽

Our Cuban family usually serves them over white rice and, sometimes when we feel particularly festive, we add chopped raw onions on top!

Disfruté!

- Michael

If Cincinnati is the Queen City, then the Cincinnati Flower Show has grown to be one of the most prized jewels in its crown.

The Show, which celebrates its 15th anniversary in 2004, has hosted some three-quarters of a million visitors and has been christened the "king of all flower shows" by *Better Homes and Gardens* magazine. It is the first and only North American show endorsed by the Royal Horticultural Society, (RHS), presenter of the prestigious Chelsea Flower Show in England.

The Show is treasured by Greater Cincinnatians and is a favorite destination for visiting gardeners. Nearly 500 zip codes are represented among the Show's visitors, according to the Society's records.

The Show's history is one of growth that would do any of its gardening participants proud.

▲ THE CASCADING FOUNTAIN, ADORNED WITH FLOWERS AT AULT PARK, THE ORIGINAL LOCATION OF THE FLOWER SHOW.

It has its beginnings in 1989, as a gleam in the eyes of then Cincinnati Park Board Director Jack Wilson and Mary Margaret Rochford, Cincinnati Horticultural Society president. The idea of a spring floral exhibition at Ault Park in Eastern Cincinnati piqued the Park Board's attention.

From the beginning, the Show's planners were thinking on the grand scale. They wanted a floral extravaganza that would rank with the great shows of the world. "We wanted to reclaim Cincinnati's prominence as a great horticulture center and create a signature event," says Mary Margaret Rochford.

So Ms. Rochford and Wilson visited the much heralded Chelsea Flower Show in London and enlisted Stephen Bennett, director of shows for the Royal Horticultural Society, and R. Ashley Stephenson, then Bailiff of the Royal Parks, as advisors to ensure a proper foundation for the Cincinnati Show.

In December of 1989, the Cincinnati Flower and Garden Show Society (now the Cincinnati Horticultural Society) was founded.

At the helm of the new not-for-profit Society's board was Martha Seaman, gardener and volunteer. The founding board of trustees were David Altman, William Baechtold, John Baumann, Ray Carr, Ted Emmerich, David Herriman, Marlene Holwadel, George Irwin, Jim King, Susan Laffoon, Margie Rauh, Phyllis Smale and Wilson.

The Society dedicated itself to the promotion of the environmental, aesthetic and educational benefits of parks and green spaces, and to providing opportunities for the enjoyment and appreciation of nature and horticulture. The Cincinnati Park Board assisted with the Society's inception and continues to support both the Society and the Flower Show.

Among the Society's first order of business: Planning for an April, 1990, debut of the Cincinnati Flower Show.

WITH OVER 20,000 VISITORS THE FIRST YEAR, THE ANNUAL SHOW CONTINUES TO DRAW LARGE CROWDS AND EARNS RAVE REVIEWS.

Just four months later, the first Cincinnati Flower Show debuted with 200 local exhibits. Set in the terraced lawns of Ault Park with its commanding pavilion, the three-day show featured gleaming white tents filled with installations and specimens provided by amateur and professional gardeners. That first year brought 20,000 visitors, rave reviews and a determination to improve and expand.

The 1991 Show brought national exhibitors and international judges; the 1992 Show saw the arrival of international exhibitors.

In its fourth year, 1993, the Show garnered international attention when it was granted the coveted endorsement of the Royal Horticultural Society, the first such recognition given a show outside England since the RHS was founded in 1804.

As the years passed, the Cincinnati Flower Show expanded to four days (1994), then five days (1996). It currently bestows exhibitor awards from the Royal, American, Chicago, Pennsylvania and Cincinnati Horticultural Societies. Hundreds of volunteers have helped the Society's staff keep the Show to running smoothly; an impressive list of businesses have provided money and in-kind support. Provident Bank has partnered since 1993 as the Show's Presenting Sponsor.

MARY MARGARET ROCHFORD ENSURES EVERYTHING IS IN PLACE FOR ANOTHER SUCCESSFUL SHOW.

Over the years, visitors have seen and gathered ideas from a series of spectacular installations in the Show's Grand Marquee. Amateur gardeners and professional florists also bring their best to be judged and admired inside, while strollers take in container gardens and overflowing window boxes outside.

The Show's Lecture Series always draws capacity crowds. The parade of speakers has included: Home and garden maven Martha Stewart, British plantswomen Penelope Hobhouse and the late Rosemary Verey, and craftswoman and children's book author Tasha Tudor.

Garden-inspired shopping for Show patrons has burgeoned. The Marketplace offers ready-to-be-planted specimens, handcrafted products from regional, national and international artisans and more than 100 vendors of garden-related items who come from more than 30 states and abroad.

MARTHA STEWART, WAS JUST ONE OF THE MANY DISTINGUISHED LECTURE SERIES' SPEAKERS APPEARING OVER THE YEARS

So, it is no surprise then that the Cincinnati Flower Show has basked in national media attention with appearances in *House Beautiful, Country Living GARDENER, Elle Decor, Country Living Home, Fine Gardening, National Geographic Traveler, USA Today* and *The New York Times*. "Good Morning America" and "CBS This Morning" have broadcast from the Show and Home & Garden Television produced a one-hour special.

The spring of 2003 marked another milestone for the Cincinnati Flower Show. The extravaganza moved east and south, locating its new home on the banks of Lake Como at historic Coney Island. The Show's theme, "Growing Together," was apt, with success having made the finite parking and space at Ault Park a limiting factor. It was time to move to a place where the Show could continue to grow.

"The Coney Island location will be able to take the Show into the future. Installing permanent gardens, instituting riverboat trips from downtown to the Flower Show and offering educational programs throughout the year are a few of the Society's goals," said Marsha Haberer, chairman of the Horticultural Society.

2003, THE FLOWER SHOW'S NEW HOME ON THE BANKS OF LAKE COMO AT HISTORIC CONEY ISLAND

The 2003 show, which attracted a crowd of more than 55,000, the largest ever, featured the Ohio Pavilion and a 1950's country garden that paid tribute to

Ohio's Bicentennial. Also introduced was the Artist's Studio with nature-inspired works by regional artists. The Show's honorary guest and lecturer was Sir Richard Carew Pole, president of the Royal Horticultural Society.

Presaging the move to Coney Island, a landmark since the 1870's, was the introduction of An Autumn Celebration in the fall of 1999. This Horticultural Society effort celebrates health, harvest and horticulture. The September 2000 Fall Flower Show at Coney Island built on its predecessor, offering family friendly exhibits and activities.

SIR RICHARD CAREW POLE, PRESIDENT OF THE ROYAL HORTICULTURAL SOCIETY, ENTERTAINS GUESTS AT THE OPENING NIGHT GALA.

The 2001 Fall Show was canceled in the wake of the 9/11 tragedies in New York and Washington DC. Instead, the Society displayed a memorial floral tribute at Cincinnati's Oktoberfest and donations were sent to the New York Fireman's Relief Fund.

In October of 2002 the Fall Flower and Farm Fest was back with earlier favorites and, as is the practice of Society planners, always with something new and always something exciting and always a great deal to delight the eye.

Carole L. Philipps

The 2004 Flower Show will be held April 21 – 25 at Coney Island.

Sweet Fields Do Lie Forgot ▶
SPONSOR: JACK ROUSE & ASSOCIATES,
ARTIST: JACK ROUSE & ASSOCIATES

1829 TO MID-1860s
LATER: THE COURT ST. MARKET
CINCINNATI, OHIO

COURT ST. MARKET

"SWEET FIELDS DO LIE FORGOT"
Andrew Marvell (a 1681)
JACK ROUSE
ASSOCIATES

In my garden there is a large place for sentiment.

My garden of flowers

is also my garden of thoughts and dreams.

The thoughts grow as freely

as the flowers, and the dreams are as beautiful.

— ABRAM L. URBAN

Dinner on the Square ▶

SPONSOR: H.B., E.W. & F.R. LUTHER FOUNDATION, FIFTH
THIRD BANK, CO-TRUSTEE, ARTIST: BONNIE RETTIG

Salads

MARY JO BECK
Children's Potting Program Chairperson and
1997 Volunteer of the YeaR

Chicken Spinach Salad

3   chicken breasts, cooked and cubed
2 cups   green grape halves
1 cup   snow peas
2 cups   spinach leaves (baby)
2 1/2 cups celery
7 oz.   corkscrew pasta or elbow macaroni, cooked and drained
6 oz.   marinated artichoke hearts, drained and quartered
1/2   large cucumber, sliced
3   green onions with tops, sliced (optional)
         large spinach leaves optional for garnish
         orange slices, optional

DRESSING:

1/2 cup   vegetable oil
1/4 cup   sugar
2 tbsp.   white wine vinegar
1 tsp.   salt
1/2 tsp. dried minced onion
1 tsp.   lemon juice
2 tbsp.   minced fresh parsley

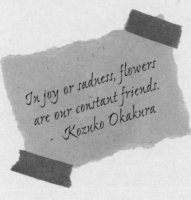

In joy or sadness, flowers are our constant friends.
- Kozuko Okakura

JEAN-ROBERT DE CAVEL
Owner, Jean-Robert at Pigall's

Crab Salad with Grapefruit and Avocado, Coulis of Mango
and Melon Balsamic Dressing

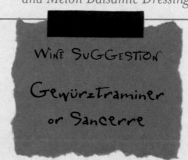

WINE SUGGESTION

Gewürztraminer
or Sancerre

12 oz.	crab meat
2	grapefruits
1	small red onion
1	mango
2	avocados
1/2	cantaloupe melon
1 cup	grapefruit juice
2 tbsp.	ketchup
4 tbsp.	mayonnaise
1 splash	brandy
2 oz.	sugar
	balsamic vinegar, extra virgin olive oil, salt and pepper

Bon Appétit,

STEP 1: MISE EN PLACE
- Peel grapefruit skin, take supreme out and squeeze juice
- Julienne grapefruit skin and blanch 3 times. Cover with water and sugar, cook slowly until candied. Keep aside.
- Reduce grapefruit juice until syrup.
- Dice red onion, keep aside.
- Make 18 avocado balls (Parisian scoop) dice the rest. Keep aside.
- Make small melon balls (Bourgeois scoop), keep aside.
- Mix ketchup and mayonnaise, splash of brandy, salt and pepper to taste.

STEP 2: PROGRESSION
- Peel and take meat from the mango. Make purée in blender, add the juice from grapefruit. Salt and pepper to taste. Keep cold.
- Keep 6 supremes of grapefruit and dice the rest.
- In a bowl mix crab meat, onion, grapefruit and diced avocado. Add sauce, salt and pepper to taste.
- Add melon to grapefruit reduction and balsamic vinegar. Salt and pepper to taste.

STEP 3: READY TO EAT
- Place mango coulis on a plate.
- Put crab salad in presentation ring and place in center of plate. Remove ring add 3 avocado balls around, add one segment of grapefruit on top and place melon dressing and candied grapefruit on top. Serve chilled.

Serves 6 ❀

GENE GOLDSCHMIDT
The Horseradish King

Auntie Ing's Potato Salad

10 Yukon Gold or 20-25 Russian Banana potatoes
3 hard boiled eggs

Cooking is like love. It should be entered into with abandon or not at all.
— Harriet Van Horne

Sometimes you need to move the duck to dig the potatoes.
— Gene

Mash egg yolks. Add 2 cups mayonnaise, 6 tbsp. Mr. Gene Greens Jalapeno Mustard, 3 tsp. Mr. Gene Greens Horseradish and beat well(more or less to taste). Chop large bunch of dill and handful of parsley(or sliced black olives, capers, etc.). Add to dressing with cubed egg whites and add potatoes. Mix well.

Serves 2 teenage boys ✤

WAYNE TIEDGE
CHS Friend

Cora's Pasta Salad

---

1 lb.   cooked spaghetti (drained)
1   cucumber diced
2   tomatoes diced (added prior to serving)
1   onion diced
1   green pepper diced
1   large bottle Wishbone Italian Dressing
1   bottle McCormick's Salad
      Supreme Seasoning
1   small jar diced small green olives
      (optional)

Mix all ingredients and refrigerate overnight,
except add tomatoes prior to serving.

Serves 8–10 ❊

**Cruise-zinnia in
Your Cadli-lilac**
SPONSOR: THOMSON
MACCONNELL CADILLAC,
INC., ARTIST: BEV KIRK

Garden of Eden
SPONSOR: HISTORIC
PROPERTIES MANAGEMENT,
ARTIST: BARBARA TRAUTH

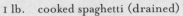

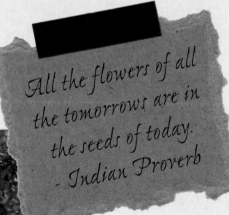

*All the flowers of all
the tomorrows are in
the seeds of today.
– Indian Proverb*

**Chrysantha"mommie
Dearest"**
SPONSOR: STEPHEN
BIRMINGHAM, ARTIST:
JUDY ANDERSON

BEVERLY A. MUSSARI

Herb Society Flower Show Volunteer
and Exhibitor

Orange-Onion-Herb-Salad with Orange Earl Grey Tea

6   oranges sliced or chunked (*remove peel)
1   large sweet or Vadalia onion sliced thin
    (other fruits can be added--blueberries, raspberries,
    watermelon or honey dew.)

DRESSING:

  6 tbsp.   olive oil
  3 tbsp.   vinegar
1/2 clove garlic minced
  2 tbsp.   honey
  2 tbsp.   basil (dried)
  2 tbsp.   oregano
  1 tbsp.   celery seed

*Before peeling orange use a zester and make
orange zest for garnish.

Mix all ingredients for dressing. Add onions and oranges. Chill. Serve on a
lettuce leaf. Use as a main salad or a side dish with Italian meals. Garnish with
fresh basil and oregano and orange zest.

For added taste and fragrance rub fresh basil over salad or serving dishes.

Serves 4-6 ❀

ORANGE EARL GREY TEA:

4-6 cups water boiled
    4-6   Earl Grey tea bags
2-3 cups orange juice
Fresh basil
Orange rinds

*Cooking is at once child's play and
adult joy. And cooking done with care
is an act of love.*
    - Craig Claiborne

Steep for three minutes, remove bags, cool. Add 1/2 cup of orange juice for
each cup of tea. Garnish with basil ice cubes. When making ice cubes add a
basil leaf and a thin slice of orange rind to each one.

Asian Carrot Salad

[OF COOKING]

"It's the company that counts—relax"
— *Miggie*

1 lb.	carrots
1 tsp.	salt
2 tbsp.	Japanese rice wine vinegar
2 tbsp.	sugar
1 tsp.	sesame oil
	salt to taste
2 tbsp.	chopped fresh cilantro or substitute fresh basil, chives, scallions or parsley

Peel the carrots and shred in a food processor (or grate by hand). Mix carrots with salt and put in a colander to drain. Let them stand for as long as you can — 20 minutes to an hour is good.

Rinse with cold water, squeeze with your hands or press with a wooden spoon to get as much water out as possible. Stir vinegar, sugar and oil together until sugar is dissolved. Mix with carrots and herbs. Add salt if needed. ❀

Tip on Gardening
Mulch to keep our plants cold — about the time Mirror Lake freezes for ice skaters.

GRANDMA'S SALAD DRESSING:

Especially good on vegetable-type salads and cottage cheese!

1 1/2 cups	oil (not olive as this is refrigerated)
1 cup	vinegar cider
1 cup	sugar
1 can	condensed tomato soup
1 tbsp.	dry mustard
1 tbsp.	paprika
1 tsp.	salt

Combine all in blender for 1 minute. Refrigerate. ❀

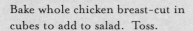

CHARLIE LUKEN
Mayor, City of Cincinnati

Sesame Chicken Salad

Bake whole chicken breast-cut in cubes to add to salad. Toss.

1	head chopped broccoli (tops only)
1	head Napa cabbage
5-6	green onions, chopped
2	packages of Ramen noodles, oriental flavored, crushed
1/2 cup	sesame seeds
1/2 cup	slivered almonds
1/4 cup	olive oil with a tablespoon melted, cooled butter

In the hope of reaching the moon men fail to see the flowers that blossom at their feet.
– Albert Schweitzer

DRESSING:

1/2 cup	olive oil
2 tsp.	soy sauce
1/2 cup	sugar
1/4 cup	red wine vinegar with garlic

Toss Together – ENJOY! ✿

▲ MAYOR LUKEN, AT LEFT, HELPS OPEN THE FLOWER SHOW.

BARBARA BUSHMAN
Flower Show Volunteer Chairperson
and 1996 Volunteer of the Year

Pasta and Feta Cheese Salad

1/2 cup	olive oil
6	garlic cloves, flattened with side of knife
8 oz.	spinach linguine
8 oz.	linguine
4	large tomatoes, seeded and chopped
1 cup	crumbled feta cheese
1/2 cup	fresh herbs, basil or oregano

▲ BARBARA AND JIM BUSHMAN

Heat oil in small skillet over medium heat. Add garlic cloves and sauté for 3 minutes. Pour mixture into small bowl. Let stand for 30 minutes. Discard garlic. Cook both pastas in large pot of boiling water until tender but still firm to the bite! Drain. Transfer pasta to a large bowl.

Add garlic oil, tomatoes, feta cheese and herbs. Toss to coat. Salt and pepper to taste and serve.

Serves 4 ❀

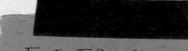

Thoughts on The Flower Power exhibit...
The Flower Power exhibit was certainly a plus for the city of Cincinnati thanks to the efforts of the Cincinnati Horticultural Society. I loved the combination of the artists' skills and the coordinated effort made to fill each pot with the perfect fit of flowers and plants.

Fresh herbs from my garden pots add that special touch to make

DENISE KUPRIONIS
Chairman of the YWCA

Denise's Caesar Salad

	Romaine lettuce – large head
	Loaf of Italian bread
1/2 cup	olive oil
1+	clove(s) garlic
1	small package anchovy fillets
2 tbsp.	fresh lime juice
2 tbsp.	Worcestershire sauce
1/2-1 tsp.	dry mustard
1	egg
dash	salt
dash	pepper
dash	garlic powder
1/2 cup+	Parmesan cheese
1/2 cup+	blue cheese

DO AHEAD:
Clean the lettuce. Tear into bite size pieces, wrap in paper towels. Store in large baggy in the refrigerator.

Make croûtons. Cube bread and place on baking pan. Sprinkle with olive oil and garlic powder. Broil for 3 or 4 minutes. Watch closely, turning occasionally. When cool, store in baggy.

Make dressing. Combine the ingredients below, shake and refrigerate:

1/2 cup	olive oil
1	clove of garlic
	dash of salt & dash of pepper
1/2-1 tsp.	mustard
	anchovies (cut up into very small pieces, including juice)
2 tbsp.	Worcestershire sauce
2 tbsp.	lime juice

RIGHT BEFORE SERVING:
Boil egg three minutes. Cool under running water. Scoop egg into dressing. Shake.

Combine: lettuce, croûtons, Parmesan cheese, blue cheese. Pour dressing over the salad. (You'll probably have more dressing than you need.) ❊

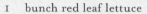

SHANNON CARTER
President and Founder, Crayons to Computers

Mullane's Salad

1   bunch red leaf lettuce
1   bunch watercress, stems removed
1/2 cup   chopped fresh basil
1 cup   feta cheese chunks
2   tomatoes cut into wedges
1/2 cup   pitted black olives
1 cup   artichoke hearts, halved
1 cup   grilled teriyaki chicken strips (optional)

Artfully arrange all ingredients in a bowl. Serve with curried yogurt dressing.

DRESSING:
1 cup   Hellman's mayonnaise
1 cup   plain yogurt
2 tsp.   teriyaki sauce
1 tbsp.   curry powder
1/4 tsp.   chopped garlic
1/2 tsp.   poppy seeds
pinch   ginger

Combine all ingredients. Serves 4 ❧

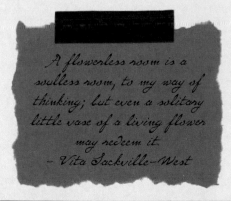

A flowerless room is a soulless room, to my way of thinking; but even a solitary little vase of a living flower may redeem it.
— Vita Sackville-West

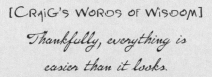

CRAIG SUMMERS BLACK
Senior Garden Editor, Better Homes and Gardens
Flower Show Judge and Speaker

Margi Pasta Salad

1	bunch basil, coarse-chopped
6-8	cloves garlic, finely chopped
3/4 can	(6 oz.) black olives, quartered
3/4 cup	pine nuts, toasted
3/4-1 cup	hydrated sun-dried tomatoes, quartered
2-3	ripe Roma tomatoes, seeded and chopped
3/4 box	(1 lb.) of thin spaghetti, fettuccine, or noodles of your choice
1/4 cup	olive oil
	fresh Parmesan cheese
	salt and pepper

[CRAIG'S WORDS OF WISDOM]
Thankfully, everything is easier than it looks.

Combine basil, garlic, black olives, pine nuts, sun-dried tomatoes and Roma tomatoes in a large serving bowl. Cook the pasta, strain well, and add to the bowl with the other ingredients. Drizzle all over with olive oil. Toss everything together, adding just enough olive oil to keep noodles from bunching together. Sprinkle fresh grated Parmesan cheese, ground pepper, and serve. ❊

▲ CRAIG WITH BARB HILDEBRANDT AND KATIE FITZGERALD

"With fronds like these, who needs anemonies?" -Craig

Leslie

LESLIE DEMORET
Flower Show Volunteer

Spinach Salad with Berries and Curry Dressing

6 oz.	fresh spinach (6 cups) pieces
1 cup	thickly sliced strawberries
1 cup	blueberries
1	small red onion, thinly sliced
1/2 cup	chopped pecans

DRESSING:

2 tbsp.	balsamic vinegar
2 tbsp.	rice vinegar
1 tbsp.	light honey + 1 tsp.
1 tsp.	curry powder
2 tsp.	Dijon mustard
	salt & pepper to taste

Wash and dry spinach. Whip together dressing ingredients. Add to spinach and toss lightly. Add berries, onion & pecans. Toss lightly and serve.

Serves 6 ❋

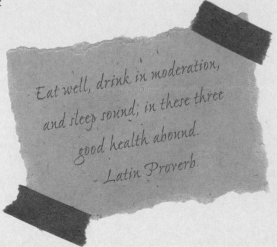

Eat well, drink in moderation, and sleep sound; in these three good health abound.

- Latin Proverb

MARIANNE MILLER

Flower Show Volunteer and President,
Association of Volunteers CHC

Swordfish Pasta Salad with Béarnaise Mayonnaise

1 1/2   swordfish steaks (3/4 to 1 inch thick)
4 tbsp.   fresh lemon juice
1/4 cup   Hellmann's mayonnaise
1 lb.   spaghetti cooked al dente and drained
1/4 cup   olive oil
1 cup   pitted and sliced black olives
1 1/2 cups pecan halves, toasted in a 350 degree oven for ten
           minutes
Béarnaise mayonnaise (see recipe)
Fresh dill and tarragon sprigs for garnish

TO PREPARE SWORDFISH:

Preheat broiler. Sprinkle swordfish on both sides with 1 tablespoon lemon juice. Spread one side of steaks with half of Hellmann's mayonnaise. Broil the steaks mayonnaise side up. Six inches from heat about five minutes. Turn steaks over spread with remaining mayonnaise and broil until done about 3-4 minutes. Let fish cool and cut into 1/2-inch cubes

Then, toss the pasta with remaining 3 tablespoons of juice and olive oil. Add olives, pecans, and swordfish and toss together.

None can have a healthy love for flowers unless he loves the wild ones.

— Forbes Watson

BÉARNAISE MAYONNAISE:

2	shallots minced
1/2 cup	dry white wine
1/4 cup	white wine vinegar
2 tbsp.	dried tarragon
2 tbsp.	dried dill
2	egg yolks
2 tbsp.	fresh lemon juice
2 tsp.	tarragon mustard
1 cup	vegetable oil
1/2 cup	olive oil
	salt and freshly ground pepper to taste

It is always exciting
to open the door and go
out into the garden
for the first time on any day.
— Marion Cran

Heat shallots, wine, vinegar, tarragon and dill to boiling in a small saucepan. Cook until almost all liquid has evaporated. Remove from heat. Process the egg yolks, lemon juice and mustard in a food processor for ten seconds. With machine running, add the oils, in a thin steady stream through the feed tube to make a thick mayonnaise. Turn off processor and add reduced shallot mixture. Process just until blended. Season to taste with salt and pepper. Makes two cups. Toss mayonnaise with pasta mixture. Garnish with fresh dill and tarragon. Refrigerate several hours to allow flavors to blend. Serve cold or let it come to room temperature.

Serves 6 ❧

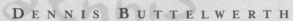

DENNIS BUTTELWERTH

Owner, Buttelwerth's, Florists Extraordinaire and
Flower Show Volunteer

Penne, Roma Tomato, and Basil Salad with Asiago Cheese

8	Roma tomatoes, quartered
8 oz.	goat cheese, crumbled
1 tbsp.	minced garlic
1 cup	basil leaves, julienned
1 cup	olive oil
2 1/2 tsp.	salt
1/2 tsp.	black pepper
1 1/2 lbs.	penne pasta
2 cups	freshly grated Asiago cheese

"To do one's best is the ultimate
of human achievement."
—Dennis

[On Cooking]
I'm a firm believer that
the best thing made in any
kitchen is a reservation.

Combine the tomatoes, goat cheese, garlic,
basil, olive oil, 1/2 teaspoon salt and pepper
in a large bowl. Prepare at least 2 hours
ahead or the day before. If made the day
before and refrigerated, bring the mixture
back to room temperature before adding
the pasta.

Bring 5 quarts of water to boil with a dash
of oil and 2 teaspoons of salt. Add the
penne pasta and cook until tender. Drain
and toss with the tomato-basil mixture.
Serve at once with the Asiago cheese.

Serves 6-8 ❀

JANET MEAKIN POOR

Former Chairman of the Board, Chicago
Horticultural Society and Flower Show Judge

Avocado–Endive Delight

4-5 tbsp.	olive oil
1 1/2 tbsp.	Dijon mustard
2	freshly squeezed lemons
3/4 tsp.	sea salt
1/2 tsp.	fresh ground pepper
4	ripe avocados, peeled and seeded
5	heads of endive

Create vinaigrette by whipping the olive oil, mustard,
lemon, salt and pepper together. Cut avocados into
large wedges. Remove the end of endives–discard
core–cut each across to one inch chunks. Lightly toss
the avocados, endive and vinaigrette. *Option:* Add
your favorite seafood: shrimp, crabmeat or lobster ❀

▲ GARY KOLLER WITH JANET

*An elegant, delicious
and easy delight! - Janet*

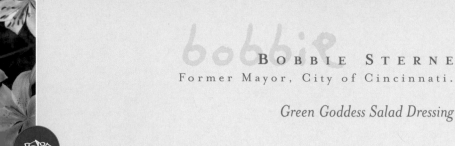

BOBBIE STERNE
Former Mayor, City of Cincinnati.

Green Goddess Salad Dressing

SALADS

1	clove garlic grated
3 tbsp.	finely chopped anchovies or anchovy paste
3 tbsp.	finely chopped chives
1 tbsp.	lemon juice
3 tbsp.	tarragon vinegar
1/2 cup	heavy sour cream
	salt and coarsely ground pepper

Combine ingredients in order given, chill thoroughly, then pour over mixed greens. Toss until well coated, adding more salt and pepper as needed. Include watercress and French endive, if you wish. Slice avocado over top. (Optional) ❈

This came from The Palace Court Hotel
sixty or seventy years ago.
It was my mother-in-law's recipe.
— Bobbie

MARY JO BECK

Children's Potting Program Chairperson
and 1997 Volunteer of the Year

Spicy Orange Salad

Visual Impressions
SPONSOR: KINGS HIGH
SCHOOL, ARTISTS: KINGS
HIGH SCHOOL STUDENTS

I cup   water
I stick   cinnamon
8   whole cloves
I   package (3 oz.) orange-
       flavored gelatin
3/4 cup   frozen orange juice concentrate
       thawed and undiluted (6 oz.)
I tbsp.   lemon juice
I can   mandarin oranges, drained (II oz.)

In saucepan, combine water, cinnamon and
cloves; bring to a boil. Reduce heat; simmer 10
minutes. Remove spices. Add dry gelatin; stir
until dissolved. Add orange juice concentrate
and lemon juice; mix well. Chill until slightly
thickened, about one hour.

**The Importance
of Being Urnest**
SPONSOR: NEYER MARKETING
PARTNERS & THE TOM NEYER
FAMILY, ARTIST: JUDY ANDERSON

Fold in mandarin oranges. Pour into 3-cup
mold, square pan or serving bowl. Chill until
firm, at least four hours.

4-6 servings ✿

*This is a holiday favorite at
our house! -Mary Jo*

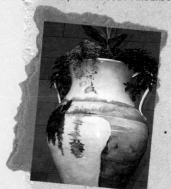

Springtime
SPONSOR: THE PATRICIA A.
VANCE FOUNDATION AND
THE WOMEN'S COMMITTEE
OF THE CINCINNATI ART
MUSEUM, ARTIST: HOLLY
SCHAPKER

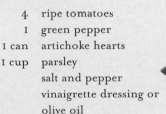

STONA & BARBARA FITCH

Former CHS Chairman and Long-Time
Community Volunteers

Garden Platter

[MY GARDENING TIP]
*I use fresh basil for this dish.
I grow it in a pot all summer and
bring it in to a sunny window when it gets
cold. I even carry my basil pot to Sanibel
and bring it back home.*

4 ripe tomatoes
1 green pepper
1 can artichoke hearts
1 cup parsley
    salt and pepper
    vinaigrette dressing or
    olive oil

Zip the skins off four tomatoes by holding them in boiling water for 15 seconds, then plunging them into ice water. Slice tomatoes into generous rounds. Line a pretty platter with torn lettuce. Place tomato slices on lettuce. Seed and slice in thin circles one green pepper, and place it on tomatoes. Add artichoke hearts cut in half to the platter. Snip about a cup of parsley on top. Season well with salt and freshly ground pepper. Drizzle the whole platter with your favorite vinaigrette dressing or just plain olive oil.

Let the whole platter sit at room temperature for a while. Enjoy! ❀

*We love fresh tomatoes. This is a beautiful way
to use fresh tomatoes either in Cincinnati in
the summer or in Florida in the winter.
- Barbara*

Vista Grand Ranch

Asian Buffalo Salad

12 oz.	buffalo rib eye, cut 1-inch thick
1	fresh jalapeno pepper, seeded and finely chopped*
1/2 tsp.	finely shredded lime peel
3 tbsp.	lime juice
2 tbsp.	reduced-sodium soy sauce
1 tbsp.	snipped fresh cilantro
2 tsp.	toasted sesame oil
1 tsp.	sugar
2	cloves garlic, minced
6 cups	salad greens, Napa cabbage and/or bok choy, 1/2
	fresh pea pods, bean sprouts
	carrots

Place steak on the unheated rack of a broiler pan. Broil 3 to 4 inches from the heat for 12 to 15 minutes or to desired doneness. Let steak stand for 5 minutes. Cut across the grain into thin bite-size strips. Meanwhile, in a medium mixing bowl stir together jalapeño pepper, lime peel, lime juice, soy sauce, cilantro, sesame oil, sugar, and garlic. Stir in beef. Marinate in the refrigerator for 2 to 8 hours. To serve, in a salad bowl toss together Napa cabbage and/or bok choy, sweet pepper or pea pods, and green onions. Stir beef mixture; arrange in center of cabbage mixture.

Prep Time: 35 minutes ❀

Cynthia

CYNTHIA SHEAKLEY MUHLHAUSER
Flower Show Volunteer

Radiatore Chicken Salad

1	package radiatore or pipe rigate pasta
2 cups	cooked chicken torn into pieces
8 oz.	cooked bacon, crumbled
1 cup	spinach leaves, washed/julienned
1/2 cup	med. size ripe olives, halved
8 oz.	deli jack cheese ,shredded
4 oz.	deli gorgonzola cheese crumbled

VINAIGRETTE:

1 tsp.	dijon mustard
1/2 cup	tarragon vinegar
1 1/2 cups	olive oil
3/4 tsp.	salt
1/2 tsp.	pepper
1/4 tsp.	sugar
1/2 tsp.	garlic powder

[CYNTHIA'S WORDS OF WISDOM]
A healthy sense of humor goes a long way when one finds themselves in unfortunate circumstances!!

Whisk together mustard and vinegar. Slowly whisk in oil, salt, pepper, sugar, and garlic powder. Cook pasta, drain, rinse with cold water. Combine pasta w/ ingredients, toss lightly with vinaigrette to coat salad.

Serves 6-8 ✳

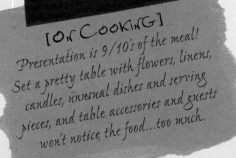

[ON COOKING]
Presentation is 9/10's of the meal! Set a pretty table with flowers, linens, candles, unusual dishes and serving pieces, and table accessories and guests won't notice the food...too much.

[ON FLOWER POWER]
Another wonderful thing that shows the creativity of the Cincinnati community.

DAVID COOK
Chef, Daveed's

Seasonal Young Greens with Taggiasca Olive Mousse, Fresh Montrachet and Fennel Saba Reduction

GREENS:

1 gal. mix of arugula, lolla rossa, frisse, oak leaf
25   taggiasca olive, stoned
3/4 cup   crème fraiche
6   1 1/2 oz. slices fresh montrachet

Wash greens. Let dry on paper towels. Refrigerate for later use. In a food processor, purée olives until smooth. Add crème fraiche. Refrigerate.

FENNEL CONFIT:

1   bulb fennel
1   Vidalia onion
1 1/2 cups   olive oil

Dice fennel and onion. Lightly simmer over low flame in olive oil until very tender. Set aside.

SABA REDUCTION:

1/2 cup   saba or balsamic vinegar
1/4 cup   extra virgin olive oil
2 tbsp.   Dijon mustard
1/2   lemon juiced
salt & pepper to taste

Combine balsamic vinegar, Dijon mustard and lemon juice. Slowly whisk in extra virgin olive oil until emulsified. ❁

▲ DAVID AND LIZ COOK

SHARON WARE
Flower Show Volunteer

Spinach Salad

1 lb	fresh spinach, cleaned, cut up and drained
1 can	(16 oz.) bean sprouts, drained
8 slices	bacon, cooked and crumbled
3	hard boiled eggs, diced

Mix the spinach and bean sprouts. Add 1/4 recipe of Betty's Salad Dressing (follows) to the bacon and eggs. Mix the eggs & bacon with spinach and sprouts. Add remainder of dressing to salad, as wanted. ✽

BETTY'S SALAD DRESSING:

1 cup	salad oil
3/4 cup	sugar
1/3 cup	catsup
1/4 cup	vinegar
1 tsp.	Worcestershire sauce
1	medium onion
1/4 tsp.	salt

Mix all ingredients in a blender until thoroughly mixed. ✽

I'd rather have roses on my table than diamonds on my neck.
—Emma Goldman

LORI MICHAELS
CHS Board Member

Napa Cabbage Salad

1/2	head Napa cabbage
4	green onions
2 tbsp.	toasted sesame seeds
1/2 cup	toasted slivered almonds
1	package Ramen noodles (chicken) crushed

Chop cabbage fine. Combine ingredients and top with crushed Ramen noodles.

SALAD DRESSING:

Whisk together...

3 tbsp.	rice vinegar
1/2 cup	salad oil
1/2 tsp.	pepper
few drops	sesame oil

Add flavor pack from Ramen noodles. Combine ingredients and mix well. ❧

Dream big, dream very big
–Lori

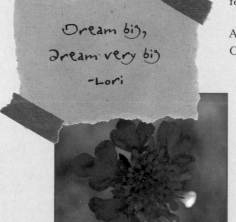

[ON GARDENING]
Love what you're doing so you'll enjoy it the most.

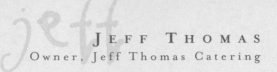

JEFF THOMAS
Owner, Jeff Thomas Catering

Grilled Italian Chicken Salad

> 6   boneless skinless chicken breasts marinated 45 minutes in:
> 2 tbsp.   red wine vinegar
> 6 tbsp.   olive oil
> 2 tsp.   garlic (minced)
> 1 tsp.   salt
> 1 tsp.   pepper
> 1 tbsp.   Italian seasonings

Grill chicken breasts two (2) minutes each side. Finish in oven 10-15 minutes at 375 degrees.

Prepare:
> 2 cups   chopped artichoke hearts
> 1/2 cup   chopped sun-dried tomatoes
> 1/2 cup   chopped green onions

Toss with cooled chicken. Add
> 3/4 cup   balsamic vinaigrette and
> 1/2 cup   grated Parmesan cheese

BALSAMIC VINAIGRETTE:
> 1/2 cup   balsamic vinegar
> 2 tbsp.   minced garlic
> 2 tbsp.   Dijon mustard
> 2 tbsp.   sugar
> 4 tbsp.   dried basil

Combine five ingredients in food processor. With processor on, slowly add 1 1/2 to 2 cups extra virgin olive oil. Season with salt and pepper.

CAESAR DRESSING:
> 4   egg yolks
> 3   anchovy fillets
> 2 tbsp.   Dijon mustard
> 2 tbsp.   minced garlic

Combine above ingredients in food processor. Slowly add 2 cups olive oil. Season with salt, pepper, and Tabasco sauce. Stir in 1/2 cup grated parmesan cheese.

Serves 6-8 people ✳

Superfast Chicken, Bacon and Tomato Salad

▲ THE CUMMINGS FAMILY

4	bacon strips, coarsely chopped
1 lb.	chicken tenders
	salt and freshly ground pepper
1/2 pint	small cherry tomatoes halved
6	scallions, white and tender green, coarsely chopped
2 tbsp.	red wine vinegar
1	large bunch watercress

Heat a large skillet. Add the bacon and cook over high heat until crisp. Transfer to a plate. Season the chicken tenders with salt and pepper, add to skillet and turn to coat with bacon fat.

This is easy and fast... a good luncheon or dinner salad.
—Claudia

Cook, turning once or twice until the tenders are brown on the outside and white throughout about five minutes. Add to the bacon.

Add the tomatoes, scallions and vinegar to the skillet and boil for 1 1/2 minutes. Return the chicken and bacon to the pan, stir well and season with salt and pepper. Arrange the watercress on 4 plates, top with the chicken salad and serve.

Delicious served with a round, ripe chardonnay!

Chicken tenders, small breast meat "tenderloins"' are widely available at supermarkets. If you can't find them, cut 1 pound of skinless, boneless chicken breasts into 2-inch wide strips. ❋

[CLAUDIA'S GARDENING TIP]
Plant markers indicating part shade/part sun— plant can only tolerate morning sun. It needs afternoon shade.
Plant markers indicating part sun/part shade—plant can tolerate either morning or afternoon sun.

CHAREE MADDUX
Owner, with husband Bob, Delhi Garden
Centers and Flower Show Exhibitor

Mandarin "Blue" Orange Salad

DRESSING:
  1/2 cup   olive oil or canola oil
    1 tsp.   salt (do not omit)
  4 tbsp.   sugar
  6 tbsp.   apple cider vinegar

Combine all ingredients in cuisinart
and then refrigerate. Shake well
before using.

SALAD:
  1/2 cup   chopped pecans
    4 tsp.   sugar
      2   medium heads of
          Boston lettuce, torn
          into bite size pieces
      1   head of iceberg lettuce,
          torn also
    1/2   red onion, thinly sliced
      1   8 oz. can mandarin
          oranges, drained
          blue cheese (optional)

▲ CHAREE AND BOB MADDUX

[ON COOKING]
*I've always loved cooking. I
started when I was 6 years old.
My grandmother and my mother-
in-law were my inspiration.*
– Charee

In small saucepan, cook pecans and sugar over medium heat until sugar is melted
and turns amber, about three to four minutes. When sugar liquifies, poor onto
waxed paper. Cool and break apart. This can be done a day ahead. Store at
room temperature.

Tear Boston and iceberg lettuce into bite size pieces. Slice red onion very thin
and put in with lettuce. Toss with dressing—you won't need to use all of it, just
enough to coat the lettuce. Add blue cheese and toss lightly. Then add mandarin
oranges and caramelized pecans.

Note: You can substitute strawberries for mandarin oranges for a change. ❀

Vice Chairman, Brunschwig & Fils, Inc. and Flower
Show Speaker 2001

Sliced Tomato Salad with Tarragon and Basil

4-6	ripe homegrown tomatoes (depending on size)
	Dijon mustard
1	garlic clove
1/4 cup	tarragon vinegar
1/2 cup	olive oil
4	scallions or 1/2 of a red onion
2 tbsp.	capers
6-8	torn fresh basil leaves
	fresh ground black pepper

Make dressing in a jam jar:

Shake 1/4 cup tarragon vinegar, 1 tablespoon Dijon mustard and 1 finely minced garlic clove until well blended. Add 1/2 cup olive oil and shake until emulsified. Put aside. Boil water in a small pan deep enough to submerge a tomato. When boiling put each individually in boiling water, count 12 seconds and remove. When tomatoes have all been processed, skin and core them and slice onto a serving platter — white or pale green.

Dice finely either 4 scallions or 1/2 red onion and sprinkle over tomatoes. Add 2 tablespoons of capers. Pour the dressing over all (as much as needed) and garnish with torn leaves of basil. Grind fresh pepper over all.

Serves 4 ❀

[Tip on Cooking]

Every late summer, when the tarragon is at its peak, I buy a dozen pint glass bottles of cider vinegar. I soak off the labels, open each bottle and jam 3 stalks of tarragon into the opening, then close the top firmly and let it steep for a week. If you then put on a lettered label — your house or garden name and the year. Voila — a lovely house gift.

Snow Pea, Peppers and Mushroom Salad

SALADS

1/2 lb.	fresh snow peas, trimmed and blanched for one minute
1/2	large yellow pepper
1/2	large red pepper
1/2 lb.	mushrooms sliced thin
2 tbsp.	sesame seeds toasted

Combine peas, peppers and mushrooms. Toss with dressing. Sprinkle with sesame seeds.

DRESSING:

2 tsp.	sesame oil
3 tbsp.	white wine vinegar
2 tbsp.	sugar
1 tsp.	ground pepper
1/4 cup	vegetable oil

◀ **House Plant**
SPONSOR: FISCHER HOMES,
ARTIST: TONYA L. MORGAN, ARTISTS' ATTIC

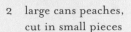

LORI OSTERHAUS
CHS Finance Manager

Marie Osterhaus' Fruit Salad

2	large cans peaches, cut in small pieces
2	medium cans pineapple tidbits
2	large cans mandarin oranges
3-4	large bananas, sliced
1	4oz. serving instant vanilla pudding
1 cup	milk
1 cup	yogurt (vanilla)
1/2 can	frozen orange juice concentrate, thawed (6 oz.)

Drain all fruit. Mix pudding with milk. Add orange juice and yogurt. Stir in fruit. Add bananas right before serving. ✻

Eating is not merely a material pleasure. Eating well gives a spectacular joy to life and contributes immensely to goodwill and happy companionship. It is of great importance to the morale.

MARGIE KYTE
Flower Show Volunteer

Oriental Pasta Salad

TOSS TOGETHER:

16 oz.	bowtie pasta, cooked al dente
1 1/2 cups	frozen sugar snap peas (whole or cut)
1/2-1 cup	thinly sliced carrots
1/2 cup	chopped red onion

MIX DRESSING:

1 tsp.	sesame seed oil (dark brown in Oriental department)
3/4 cup	oil
2 tsp.	soy sauce
3/4 cup	sugar
1/2 cup	red wine vinegar
	seasoning packets from 2 Ramen "Oriental" or "Shrimp" noodle soups

1/2	stick butter
1 cup	sliced almonds
	Ramen noodles

A light, savory combination that can be made a day ahead!
—Margie

Blend and pour most of dressing over bowtie pasta and vegetables. Refrigerate overnight or at least two hours. Melt 1/2 stick butter in skillet. Add 1 cup sliced almonds and all Ramen noodles — well broken. Brown together and fold into pasta before serving. Add rest of dressing as needed. (Add 1 1/4 lb. cooked shelled shrimp or cooked, cubed chicken if desired.)

Serves 10 ✿

JIMMY GHERARDI
Chef, J's Seafood Restaurant

Cucumber Salad

Dogs and Cat Tails
SPONSOR: HYDE PARK SQUARE,
ARTIST: CARRIE LYNN COOKE

1 cup	plain yogurt or goats milk yogurt
3-4	cloves finely minced garlic
2 tbsp.	olive oil
1 tbsp.	balsamic vinegar
1 tsp.	salt
1/2 tsp.	black pepper
2	cucumbers, peeled, seeded and cut into 1/2 inch pieces
1/4 cup	fresh mint leaves-torn

In a large bowl combine all of the ingredients except the cucumbers and mint leaves. Whisk to combine well. Refrigerate until ready to serve.

To serve: Whisk the mixture. Add the cucumbers and mint leaves. Stir to combine well. ❋

William Shakespetal
SPONSOR: KENDLE
INTERNATIONAL INC., ARTIST:
TONYA L. MORGAN,
ARTISTS' ATTIC

*Each flower is a soul
opening out to nature.
— Gerald De Nerval*

The Natural History
SPONSOR: LIGHTBORNE
COMMUNICATIONS INC.,
ARTIST: DOUGLAS P. SMITH

MARSHA HABERER
Chairman of the Board, The Cincinnati Horticultural Society

Grilled Salmon Salad with Creamy Tarragon Dressing

8	salmon fillets (6-8 oz. and about I 1/2 inches thick)
1/3 cup	soy sauce
I tsp.	grated lemon rind
1/4 cup	fresh lemon juice
I	clove garlic, minced
2 tsp.	Dijon mustard
1/2 cup	vegetable oil
12 cups	mixed salad greens

Place fillets in a large shallow dish. Combine soy sauce and next 5 ingredients, stirring well. Pour over fillets. Cover and marinate in refrigerator for 3 hours, turning once each hour.

Remove fillets from marinade, discarding marinade. Grill fillets, over medium-hot coals with grill lid closed, (350 degrees to 400 degrees) 6 minutes on each side or until fish flakes easily when tested with a fork.

To serve, place I fillet on I 1/2 cups salad greens, and top with 1/4 cup Creamy Tarragon Dressing. Garnish with fresh tarragon sprigs if desired.

Serves 8 ❁

CREAMY TARRAGON DRESSING:

2 cups	mayonnaise
1/3 cup	buttermilk
3 tbsp.	finely chopped fresh tarragon
2 tbsp.	finely chopped fresh parsley
2 tbsp.	chopped green onions
2 tbsp.	tarragon vinegar
I 1/2 tsp.	Worcestershire sauce
1/4 tsp.	dried thyme
I tsp.	sugar
I tsp.	freshly ground pepper
1/2 tsp.	salt
1/2 tsp.	hot sauce

▲ AMY SMYTHE, MARSHA AND HAZEL PARRISH

KATHLEEN BENKEN

Owner, H. J. Benken Florist and Flower Show Exhibitor

Grandma Maime's German Potato Salad

1	5 lb. bag red potatoes — cook with skins and cool
1	green or red pepper, chopped
1	medium onion, chopped
2	stalks celery, chopped
6	hard cooked eggs
1 1/2	lb. bacon, fried crisp

Remove bacon and allow grease to cool. Slice cooled potatoes. Add chopped vegetables. Add crumbled bacon. Add 1 teaspoon salt and 1/2 teaspoon pepper.

To cooled bacon grease, add: 1 1/2 cups sugar, 1 cup apple cider vinegar, 1/2 cup water. Simmer slowly, until thickened. Mix with vegetables. ❁

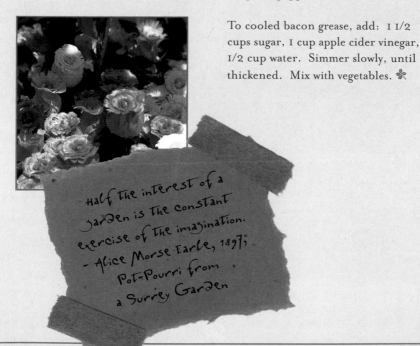

Half the interest of a garden is the constant exercise of the imagination.
— Alice Morse Earle, 1897;
Pot-Pourri from a Surrey Garden

RON L. WISE
Owner and Chef, Rondo's

Pan Fried Ciabatta Salad

8	1/2 inch slices of Ciabatta bread
4	Roma tomatoes – cut in half & oven dried
1/2	red onion thinly sliced
1/2 lb.	Gorgonzola or your favorite blue cheese
1/2	head of escarole
1/2 cup	extra virgin olive oil

Sauté Ciabatta in oil, browning on both sides. Top with oven dried tomatoes, blue cheese, red onion & escarole. Drizzle with dressing.

Serves 8 ❊

WHITE BALSAMIC FRESH GRAPE VINAIGRETTE:

1	shallot – small dice
1 cup	fresh grapes
1	clove garlic – finely minced
1/4 cup	white balsamic vinegar
1/2 tsp.	Dijon mustard
	Juice of 1/2 a lemon
1/2 cup	extra virgin olive oil
	salt & pepper to taste

Put all ingredients – except the oil, in a blender and process. Slowly adding the oil – to emulsify the dressing.

FRANCES JONES POETKER

Award Winning Floral Designer and a 1992 Great Living Cincinnatian

Dandelion Spinach Salad

1 lb.	fresh, crisp spinach
1 can	11 oz. mandarin orange segments, drained
16 to 24	dandelion buds
3 tbsp.	oil
1 tbsp.	lemon juice
1 1/2 tbsp.	vinegar
	salt and pepper

Remove stems from spinach; wash thoroughly and pat dry. Tear into bite-size pieces. Place spinach and mandarin orange segments in salad bowl. Put the dandelion buds in a separate bowl and coat with the oil, lemon juice, vinegar, salt and pepper. Add to the salad. Toss gently with the champagne dressing.

Serves 4-6 ❀

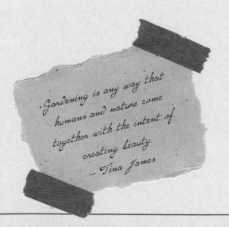

Gardening is any way that humans and nature come together with the intent of creating beauty.
— Tina James

CHAMPAGNE DRESSING:

2 cups	salad oil
3/4 cup	cider vinegar
3/4 cup	sugar
1 tsp.	celery seed
1 tsp.	dry mustard
2 tsp.	salt
1	onion cut into quarters

Blend all ingredients in blender on "mix". Store dressing in refrigerator.

Donald Breen, Jr.
CHS Friend

Rotini Salad with Basil, Parsley and Mozzarella

10 oz.	rotini pasta
2 cups	canned crushed tomatoes
1/2 cup	orange juice
2 cloves	garlic, minced
3 tbsp.	chopped fresh basil
3/4 tsp.	grated orange zest
3/4 tsp.	ground ginger
1/2 tsp.	salt
1/4 tsp.	freshly ground black pepper
2 tsp.	olive oil
6 oz.	part-skim mozzarella cheese diced (about 1 1/2 cups)
1 cup	thinly sliced celery
1 cup	diced orange segments
2 tbsp.	chopped fresh parsley

Heat a large pot of water to boiling and cook the rotini until just tender. Drain well. In a medium saucepan, combine the tomatoes, orange juice, garlic, basil, zest, ginger, salt and pepper. Bring to a boil over high heat and reduce to a simmer. Cover and cook until the garlic is tender and the flavors have blended, about 5 minutes. Remove from the heat and stir in the oil. Transfer the tomato mixture to a large serving bowl. Cool to room temperature.

Add the rotini and toss to combine. Add the mozzarella, celery, orange and parsley and toss again. Serve immediately, or cover and refrigerate up to four hours.

We All Live In A Yarrow Submarine
SPONSOR: PROVIDENT BANK,
ARTIST: DEBBIE BURGESS

Manager of the Krohn Conservatory and Flower Show
Volunteer

"Baked Potato" Potato Salad - for Baked Potato Lovers

5 lbs.	cooked red potatoes - diced
1	8 oz. sour cream
1/2 cup	mayonnaise
8 oz.	shredded cheddar cheese
1/2 lb.	cooked crumbled bacon
1	bunch of green onions - diced
	salt and pepper to taste

Boil potatoes in jackets, let cool before dicing. Set aside. Mix sour cream and mayo - set aside. Dice green onions.

Mix potatoes and sour cream and mayo mixture together until potatoes are well covered. Mix in 3/4 of cheese, 3/4 of bacon and half of the diced green onions. Salt and pepper to taste. Garnish the top with the remainder of the cheese, bacon and green onions. ❊

Who would have thought it possible that a tiny little flower could preoccupy a person so completely that there simply wasn't room for any other thought....
— Sophie Scholl

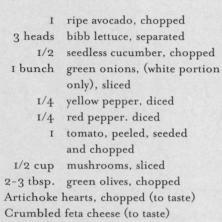

LINDA SCHLEGEL
CHS Event Manager

Vegetable Salad

1	ripe avocado, chopped
3 heads	bibb lettuce, separated
1/2	seedless cucumber, chopped
1 bunch	green onions, (white portion only), sliced
1/4	yellow pepper, diced
1/4	red pepper. diced
1	tomato, peeled, seeded and chopped
1/2 cup	mushrooms, sliced
2-3 tbsp.	green olives, chopped

Artichoke hearts, chopped (to taste)
Crumbled feta cheese (to taste)

Mix all ingredients together.

SALAD DRESSING:

4 tbsp.	red wine vinegar
12 tbsp.	olive oil
1 clove	garlic, minced
1 tsp.	Dijon mustard

Mix vinegar, mustard and garlic together. Whisk in oil. Add salt, pepper and fresh herbs to taste. Add dressing gradually to vegetables and gently toss. ❋

◀ **Mary, Mary, Clean and Airy, How Does Your Region Grow?**
SPONSOR: OHIO-KENTUCKY-INDIANA REGIONAL COUNCIL OF GOVERNMENTS, ARTIST: KATHY SABATO

KATHLEEN McNAMARA
CHS Friend

Autumn Rice Salad

2 cups	rice
4 cups	chicken broth
3	6 oz. jars artichoke hearts, chopped and juice reserved
5	green onions
1	14 oz. jar green olives, chopped
1	green pepper, sliced and diced
1/4 cup	parsley
1 tsp.	curry powder
1/2	of the reserved artichoke marinade salt and pepper to taste

Bring stock to boil, add rice, cover and simmer over low heat for 20 minutes. Let cool. Mix all ingredients with rice. Refrigerate.

Serves 8 ❊

He who is born with a silver spoon in his mouth is generally considered a fortunate person, but his good fortune is small compared to that of the happy mortal who enters this world with a passion for flowers in his soul.

— Celia Thaxter

ANN M. OTT

CHS Friend

Fresh Tomato Salad with Shells and Chicken

SALADS

2 1/2 cups	small shell pasta uncooked
4-6 cups	cut up cherry tomatoes
2 cups	(12 oz.) cooked chicken, cut into 1/2 inch cubes
2 cups	frozen green peas, thawed
1 cup	crumbled feta cheese
1 cup	sliced ripe olives
1/2 cup	sliced scallions
2/3 cup	prepared ranch dressing

Cook pasta, drain and rinse. Place in a large bowl. Slice cherry tomatoes in half. Add remaining ingredients. Toss with dressing to coat. Serve on lettuce. ✻

◀ **Cinzinnia Zoo and Potanical Gardenia**
SPONSOR: CINCINNATI ZOO AND BOTANICAL GARDENS, ARTIST: NANCY MCCARTHY AND DEBBIE LENTZ

BARBARA HARDING
Community Volunteer

Orzo, Wild Rice and Asparagus Salad

▲ BARBARA AND WARREN HARDING

1 lb.	asparagus, trimmed
1 cup	wild rice, rinsed
1 lb.	orzo pasta
1 cup	tiny frozen peas, defrosted
4	green onions, sliced
1/4 cup	diced red onion
1	red bell pepper, sliced
1/4 cup	chopped cilantro
2 tbsp.	chopped mint

VINAIGRETTE:

2 tbsp.	lemon juice
2 tbsp.	white wine vinegar
1 clove	garlic, minced
2 tsp.	Dijon mustard
	salt and pepper
1/2 cup	extra virgin olive oil

Cut asparagus diagonally into 3/4 inch slices. Blanch in boiling salted water until just tender. Drain and rinse under cold running water. Pat dry and set aside. Bring 4 cups water to a boil and season with salt. Stir in wild rice and reduce the heat. Simmer, covered, about 45 minutes. The rice should be tender but still have a little bite when tasted. Drain well.

Cook orzo according to package directions in boiling salted water. Drain and rinse under cold running water. Drain well and toss with a little olive oil to prevent sticking. Combine asparagus, wild rice, and orzo with remaining salad ingredients in a large mixing bowl. Toss well to mix.

Combine the lemon juice, vinegar, garlic, Dijon, and salt and pepper in a small bowl. Whisk in the olive oil. Taste and add more lemon juice and salt and pepper if needed. Add to salad and toss to mix well. Adjust the seasoning.

To serve, arrange a border of lettuce leaves on a platter or in a shallow bowl. Mound salad on lettuce. Recipe from Jungle Jim's cooking school.

Serves 8 ❧

NANCY AND MIKE O'CONNOR

Express Cincinnati, Friends of the Cincinnati Flower Show

Simply Delicious Spinach Salad

▲ NANCY, MIKE AND KOKI

1 large bag of fresh baby spinach, patted dry

About 6-8 small green onions with tops, thinly sliced

1 large can mandarin orange sections, drained well

About 1 cup slivered or sliced almonds, (carefully brown them very lightly under the broiler and cool them before using)

DRESSING:

Place equal amounts of honey, salad vinegar (I use tarragon vinegar) and extra virgin olive oil in a small jar and shake well to blend. A quarter cup of each is about right, but you might want to start with a quarter cup of honey and add more or less oil and vinegar to taste.

Place the spinach in a large wooden bowl and toss with onions. Garnish with oranges and toasted almonds. Drizzle dressing over the salad just before serving.

Serves 4-6. ❦

This is so simple, but it looks beautiful and has a wonderful taste. It's especially good served with creamy coq au vin style crepes or any light chicken or fish entree. I made this recipe up at home after having something like it at a restaurant, so you could easily adjust the amount of the ingredients to your own taste.

— Nancy

Chairperson of Dramatic Table Settings and
President of ACHS

Pear and Pecan Salad

Field greens
Sliced red pear
Gorgonzola cheese, crumbled
Toasted pecans

DRESSING:

1/3 cup   canola oil
3 tbsp.   red wine vinegar
3 tbsp.   sugar
          salt and pepper to taste

Place greens in a bowl. Place pear slices around
edge. Place cheese toward center and and pecans
in center of cheese. Pour dressing over top. ✻

***BoVining Pot of
Leopold's Blooms***
SPONSOR: DUBLINER
RESTAURANT, ARTIST:
HELEN RYAN

We Color the World
SPONSOR: COLOR
RESOLUTIONS INTERNATIONAL,
ARTIST:DAVID A. WILSON

Crowning Glory
SPONSOR: CINCINNATI
FLOWER SHOW,
ARTIST: ARTWORKS

KATHY ELLIOTT
Flower Show Volunteer

Fresh Corn and Cilantro Salad

6 ears corn, shucked
6-8 peppercorns
2 1/2 tbsp. chopped cilantro
1 shallot, minced
1/4 cup best quality olive oil
coarse or kosher salt

A garden is a delight to the eye and a solace for the soul.
— Sadi

Bring pot of water to boil. Add corn and boil 4-5 minutes. Drain and cool. Using a knife, scrape the kernels and squeeze any corn pulp. Place in medium bowl. Crack peppercorns (place in plastic and smash).

Mix pepper, cilantro and shallot and add to bowl. Stir in olive oil and fold to incorporate. Taste for extra seasoning and serve. ❋

◀ ***God Shed His Grace On Thee***
SPONSOR: WESTERN & SOUTHERN
FOUNDATION, ARTIST: JANELLA ALBRIGHT

JULIE WEINEL
CHS Horticulture Manager

Weinel's Wilted Watercress Salad

4	bunches fresh watercress, cleaned and chopped
1/2 lb.	bacon, diced (reserve grease)
2 tbsp.	vinegar
1/2 cup	water
1 tbsp.	sugar
2	hard boiled eggs, diced
1/3 cup	green onion, chopped

Fry bacon in skillet until crisp. Remove bacon to drain on plate lined with paper towels, reserving grease in skillet. Add vinegar, sugar and water to grease (more or less can be added to taste); whisk. Combine watercress, egg, green onion and bacon in large bowl. Pour hot grease mixture over top and gently combine.

Serves 4-5. ❊

[My Gardening Tip]

When adding new plants to your garden, consider incorporating plants that attract wildlife such as hummingbirds, yellow finches and butterflies. In my garden, Buddleia (butterfly bush) attracts hummingbirds and butterflies. Plants that develop seed heads such as sunflowers and Echinacea (coneflower) attract yellow finches. This adds an entertainment value to the garden that can be enjoyed while weeding, relaxing or hosting a family picnic.

– Julie

FRANK NEUMANN
Flower Show Volunteer

Rita Neumann's Russian Potato Salad

2 1/2	lbs. potatoes
2	large pickled cucumbers
1	medium onion
1	small apple
2 1/2 tbsp.	oil
1/2 tsp.	pepper
1 tsp.	salt
1 cup	sour cream
3/4 cup	nonfat yogurt

Boil potatoes. Keep firm. Peel and cube. Dice pickles, onion and apple.

Add all ingredients and mix well. ❊

◀ **Roto-dendron**
SPONSOR: ROTO ROOTER,
ARTIST: MICHAEL SHARP

SUSAN KELLY
Chef's Choice Catering

Tuscan Salad with Chicken and Gorgonzola

2 heads bibb lettuce
2 heads red leaf lettuce
1 head radicchio

Tear lettuce and toss.

Top with 2 cups golden raisins; 1 can roasted red peppers, in strips; 1 1/2 cups crumbled gorgonzola; 4 grilled chicken breasts, cut in strips.

DRESSING:

3/4 cup	white balsamic vinegar
1 tsp.	chopped fresh garlic
1 tsp.	chopped fresh shallot
2 tbsp.	Dijon mustard
	pinch of sugar
1 tsp.	salt
1/2 tsp.	pepper
2 tbsp.	fresh basil, chopped
2 cups	olive oil

Blend all ingredients except olive oil in processor or blender. While blending, add oil slowly until incorporated. Chill.

Drizzle dressing over topped greens. ❊

Taft Museum of Artemisia
SPONSOR: TAFT MUSEUM OF ART, ARTIST: MARLENE STEELE

Hip to be Square
SPONSOR: CINCINNATI FLOWER SHOW, ARTIST: JENNIFER WILSON

Sumo in the City
SPONSOR: FRCH DESIGN WORLDWIDE, ARTIST: FRCH DESIGN WORLDWIDE

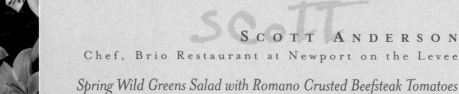

Spring Wild Greens Salad with Romano Crusted Beefsteak Tomatoes
Garnished with Edible Flowers

SALADS

BALSAMIC VINAIGRETTE:

1 1/4 cups	balsamic vinegar
1/4 cup	whole grain mustard
1 tbsp.	freshly chopped basil
1 tsp.	freshly chopped Italian parsley
1 tsp.	minced garlic
1/4 lb.	light brown sugar

Combine ingredients in a bowl. Mix well, by hand. Continue whisking while slowly drizzling in 1 quart olive oil. Hand mix until oil is completely emulsified. (Makes 1 3/4 quart and can be cut in half).

ROMANO BREADING:

4 cups	Japanese (panko) bread crumbs
2 cups	grated Romano cheese
2 tbsp.	freshly chopped parsley
1 tbsp.	cracked black pepper

Slice approximately 12 beefsteak tomatoes into 3/4 inch slices, removing core. Dredge tomato slices in flour, shaking off excess. Make egg wash of 1 part milk and one part whole egg.

Dredge slices through egg wash. Firmly press tomato slices into Romano breading until completely covered.

Heat olive oil in sauté pan until hot but not smoking. Sear tomato slice on one side, and then turn to evenly brown both sides. Remove from oil onto paper towel to drain excess oil.

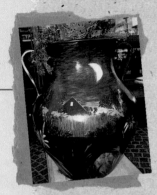

In mixing bowl toss field greens (organic mixture of arugula, red oak, frissee, radiccio and other seasonal greens) about 3 ounces by weight, with 1 tablespoon grated Asiago cheese (sharp Italian dry white), 1 –2 ounces balsamic vinaigrette and a warm grilled chicken breast thinly sliced. Top with edible flower garnish and Romano crusted tomatoes. ❋

Edible flower suggestions include rose petals, orchids, pansies and nasturtiums.

Crab and Celery Root Remoulade

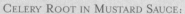

SALADS

CELERY ROOT IN MUSTARD SAUCE:

1 lb.	celery root (about 3 cups when peeled and cut)
2 tsp.	lemon juice
4 tbsp.	Dijon prepared mustard
3 tbsp.	boiling water
2 tbsp.	white wine vinegar
1/2 cup	olive oil
	salt and pepper
1	carrot peeled and grated

Peel the celery root and cut into pieces and grate in food processor (ends up looking like matchsticks). Peel and grate the carrot, place in mixing bowl with the salt, lemon juice and let it steep for about 30 minutes. Rinse the pieces of carrot with cold water in a strainer and dry them off with a towel.

Warm a mixing bowl in hot water, then dry it off. Add the mustard and beat in the boiling water in droplets with a whisk. Then beat in the oil by droplets to make a creamy sauce. Beat in the vinegar. Season to taste.

Fold in the celery root and carrot mixture into the sauce and allow it to marinate for 2-3 hours.

When ready to serve drain the sauce from mixture.

CRAB:

3 tbsp.	olive oil
2 tbsp.	white wine vinegar
1 tsp.	Dijon mustard
1 1/2 lbs.	fresh Jonah crab
1 cup	mayonnaise
4 tbsp.	chili sauce
2 cloves	garlic, crushed

Whisk together first 3 ingredients until well blended. Meanwhile whisk mayonnaise, chili sauce and garlic in small bowl. Add to above mixture. Toss in the crab.

Place the celery root mixture at the bottom of the glass about half full, then place the crab mixture on top. The crab should be mounded over the top of glass. Complete with a sprinkle of chopped parsley. ❧

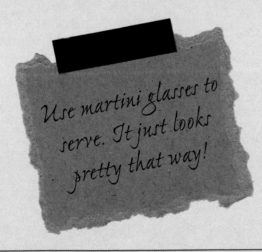

Use martini glasses to serve. It just looks pretty that way!

Tea Pot
SPONSOR: THE JOHN G. AND PHYLLIS W. SMALE FUND, ARTIST: DEIRDRE MAHNE

Joy Is Simple: Flowers of the Past
SPONSOR: AUCTIONS BY MAGGIE, INC., ARTIST: JUDY HARRELL

Carpe Diem
SPONSOR: A.J. RAHN GREENHOUSES, ARTIST: MARIAN JACKSON

SALADS

101

MARIE HUENEFELD

CHS Board Member and Flower Show Publicity Volunteer

Crabmeat Ring

APPETIZER OR INDIVIDUAL SALAD SERVINGS:

1 1/2	envelopes Knox gelatin (small envelopes)
1/2 cup	cold water
1	can (10 oz.) Campbell's tomato soup, undiluted
1	package (8 oz.) Philadelphia cream cheese, softened
1 cup	mayonnaise
2	cans crab
1 cup	finely chopped celery
1/2 cup	finely chopped onion

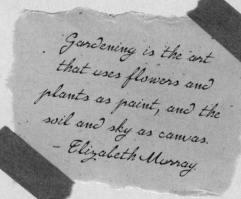

Gardening is the art that uses flowers and plants as paint, and the soil and sky as canvas.
— Elizabeth Murray

Heat tomato soup. Soften gelatin in water. Stir gelatin into tomato soup until dissolved. Mash softened cream cheese and stir until smooth. Add mayonnaise to cream cheese blending well Add mayonnaise and cream cheese mixture to tomato soup, blend well. Add crab, celery and onions. Add pinch of salt and seasoned pepper.

Pour whole mixture into moistened 1 1/2 quart mold .

TO SERVE:
Unmold and place on center of large platter. Surround with Ritz crackers. Fill center with flowers, or parsley or something colorful.

This also can be used as a salad if individual molds are used. Unmold and place on lettuce and serve as a salad.

Serves 6–8 individually or more if used as an appetizer. ✳

CHRIS MONZEL
Cincinnati City Council

Gordon's Feta Craisin Salad

DRESSING:
1/4 cup	oil (canola & olive)
1 tbsp.	balsamic vinegar
1	clove garlic
1 tsp.	Dijon mustard
1/2 tsp.	honey
	dash of salt

To make the salad dressing combine the ingredients in a jar then shake vigorously.

For the actual salad, use romaine lettuce or spinach leaves; then mix salad dressing in, then add walnut pieces, feta cheese and craisins to your liking to top it off. ❀

▲ MARY GRACE AND JACOB MONZEL

It's a great day to be alive, carpe diem, and never lose your sense of humor.

— Chris

MIKE STARKEY

Chef, Hyde Park Country Club

Lime-Chili Chicken Salad

6 oz.	chicken breast
	lime juice
	olive oil
1 tsp.	cumin
1 tbsp.	dark chili powder
	your favorite mixed greens
	fresh raspberries
	mandarin oranges
	sliced strawberries
	toasted macadamia nuts
	blackberries (if available)
	your favorite raspberry dressing

Allow chicken to marinate in lime juice, olive oil, cumin and chili powder for 24 hours.

Place your greens into a larger bowl and pour your dressing over the salad and toss well evenly coating your lettuce. Remove and place onto your plate. Sprinkle your berries atop the greens and place the oranges and macadamias accordingly. Julienne your cooked/marinated chicken around the greens and serve.

Make sure the chicken is tepid, not hot or cold. ❁

I have found, through years of practice, that people garden in order to make something grow; to interact with nature; to share, to find sanctuary, to heal, to honor the earth, to leave a mark. Through gardening, we feel whole as we make our personal work of art upon our land.
– Julie Moir Messervy

Zucchini–Stick Salad

1   small zucchini
    oil and vinegar dressing
    (I find Italian salad dressing
    to be very good.)
    leaf lettuce
    paprika

Peel and slice the zucchini into sticks.
Drain on paper toweling. Place them in
shallow container and marinate in
dressing. Serve on lettuce leaves and
garnish with paprika.

Fast, easy and tasty! The marinated
sticks can also be used as an appetizer
when served with a dip. ❁

*Even people who don't
usually like zucchini,
find this really tasty!*
— Jan

JOYCE HOLMES
Community Volunteer

Brawny Broccoli Salad

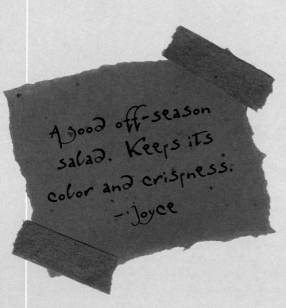

SALADS

3	large broccoli stalks (or equivalent pre-cut florets)
1/4 lb.	Swiss cheese, grated
3	green onions, chopped, including some of tops
1/2 cup	mayonnaise
1/4 cup	sugar
1 tbsp.	cider vinegar
1/2 lb.	thick cut bacon, fried crisp and crumbled

Wash broccoli bunches and cut tops into bite-size florets. (Discard stalks or reserve for alternate use). Combine florets with Swiss cheese and green onions. In small side bowl, blend together the mayonnaise, sugar and vinegar for dressing. Blend into broccoli mixture lightly. Refrigerate, letting salad marinate overnight.

Just before serving, stir in some of the crumbled bacon, reserving some to sprinkle on top.

Serves approximately 6 ❋

A good off-season salad. Keeps its color and crispness.
—Joyce

SUSAN KAHN

1994 Flower Show Gala Co-Chair

Cranberry Mousse

20 oz.	crushed pineapple
6 oz.	strawberry jello
1 cup	water
1	can whole cranberry sauce
3 tbsp.	lemon juice
2 cups	sour cream
1/2 cup	pecans

Drain pineapple, save juice. Add juice, jello and water in sauce pan. Heat to dissolve. Blend in cranberry sauce, lemon juice and chill until semi-firm. Then blend in sour cream and fold in pineapple and pecans. Chill. ✤

This is a great recipe for the holidays!

Dog Daisy Summer
SPONSOR: STANLEY M. CHESLEY,
HON. SUSAN J. DLOTT,
AND WAITE, SCHNEIDER,
BAYLESS & CHESLEY, ARTIST:
CLARA OF ABC AND E DESIGN

Haute Couture des Fleurs
SPONSOR: SAKS FIFTH AVENUE,
ARTIST: MARK ADAMS

Cassatt's Motley Pot
SPONSOR: SARA M. VANCE
AND MICHELLE WADDELL,
ARTIST: HOLLY SCHAPKER

*Principles have no
real force except when
one is well fed.*

– Mark Twain

Bluebirds of Spring ▶
Sponsor: Scripps Howard Foundation, Artist: Bev Kirk

Entrées

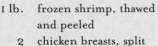

JIM KNIPPENBERG
The Cincinnati Enquirer

Chicken and Shrimp Pasta

ENTRÉES

I lb.	frozen shrimp, thawed and peeled
2	chicken breasts, split
I	medium onion, diced
1/4 cup	chopped parsley
I	can (8 oz.) tomato sauce
1/3 cup	Port wine
1/4 cup	water
3/4 tsp.	salt
I tsp.	chopped basil
1/4 tsp.	pepper

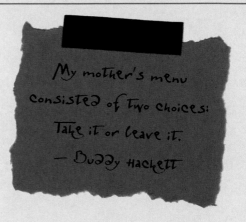

My mother's menu consisted of two choices: Take it or leave it.
— Buddy Hackett

In a 12-inch skillet over medium heat, melt butter and sauté onion until translucent; remove onion in the drippings, still over medium heat, cook the chicken through, add the cooked onion, parsley, tomato sauce, wine, water, salt, basil, pepper. Heat to a boil, reduce to low, cover and simmer 10 minutes. add the shrimp and simmer 5 more minutes. Serve over pasta of choice. ✣

brunhilde

BRUNHILDE KUNZEL,
Spouse of CSO/CPO Conductor, Maestro Erich Kunzel

Veal Rouladen on Creamed Kohlrabi

4 slices	(5 ounces each) of veal/turkey breast
4 slices	cooked ham
4	eggs, hard boiled
	salt and pepper to taste
2 tbsp.	mustard
1 oz.	butter
2 tbsp.	shallots, chopped
1 tbsp.	garlic, chopped
8	basil leaves
3/8 cup	white wine
5/8 cup	chicken stock
2	kohlrabi
5/8 cup	heavy cream
2	tomatoes, peeled, seeded and quartered
	parsley, chopped

Tulips that Lied
SPONSOR: PRIORITY DISPATCH,
ARTIST: BERNICE WOOD,
ARTISTS' ATTIC

Put meat between two sheets of plastic wrap and pound thin. Sprinkle both sides of each piece with salt and pepper. Spread mustard on just one side. Put two basil leaves on top of mustard and add a slice of ham. Put egg on top of ham. Roll each up tight and fasten with toothpicks.

Heat in butter and brown on all sides. Add shallots, garlic, wine and stock. Simmer until the meat is tender. Take out rouladen and strain the sauce. Add the cubed, peeled kohlrabi to the sauce. Add salt, pepper, and the heavy cream and cook the kohlrabi until tender. Add the quartered tomatoes and put the kohlrabi on plates. Cut the rouladen in half and put on top of the kohlrabi. Decorate with chopped parsley.

Hyde Park Square
SPONSOR: THE KILN AT HYDE
PARK SQUARE, ARTIST: KRUMME,
BROWN, LODDER, UNGERS AND
PHILPOTT

Reprinted from *Rhapsody of Recipes* by kind permission of The Friends of the Pops.

Serves 4. 🌸

Herbie Potter
SPONSOR: ASHLAND INC.
FOUNDATION, ARTIST:
ART STOP KIDS

ENTRÉES

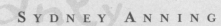

SYDNEY ANNING

Amateur Flower Show Participant and 2003
Committee Chair

Seared Mahi–Mahi with a Garlic –Sesame Crust

ENTRÉES

> 4   7 ounce mahi-mahi fillets
>   salt and peppered
> 1 1/2 cups   sesame seeds
> 5 tsp.   garlic, chopped
> 1/2 cup   unsalted butter, softened
> 3 tbsp.   olive oil

Mix sesame seeds and garlic into the softened
butter, adding salt and pepper to taste.
Spread on top of fillets to form a 1/4" crust.
Sear fillets on all sides in hot olive oil,
being careful not to overcook (about one
minute). Garnish with basil and serve with
Lime Ginger Sauce.

Serves 4 ✻

LIME GINGER SAUCE:

> 3/4 cup   dry white wine
> 2 1/2 tsp.   fresh ginger, minced
> 1/2 cup   heavy cream
> 1 cup   cold unsalted butter, cut in
>   small pieces
>   juice of one lime
>   salt and pepper

In a sauce pan, combine wine and ginger,
bring to a boil, reduce heat and cook
until reduced by 1/3. Add cream and
reduce by 1/3 again. Over low heat, add
butter slowly, one piece at a time being
careful not to let boil for it will separate.
Add the lime juice and salt and pepper.
Can be prepared ahead of time and
reheated over simmering water. Serve
with Seared Mahi-Mahi. ✻

▲ SYDNEY AND DENNIS BUTTELWERTH

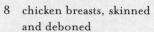

BETTY WUEST

Flower Show Chairperson and 1995 Volunteer of the Year

Sweet and Sour Chicken

8	chicken breasts, skinned and deboned
8	pineapple slices
1	small green pepper
8 oz.	Russian dressing
4 oz.	apricot preserves or orange marmalade
1 pkg.	onion soup mix
1/4 cup	water (I often use the pineapple juice)

Lay chicken breasts in baking dish, lay pineapple and green peppers on chicken breasts.

Mix Russian dressing, preserves, soup mix and water. Pour mix over chicken breasts.

Cover with foil, bake at 350 degrees for 1 hour. Remove foil, bake for another 1/2 hour.

Serve over cooked rice. ✳

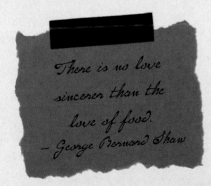

There is no love sincerer than the love of food.
– George Bernard Shaw

GARY KOLLER
Flower Show Judge

Spice-Brined Pork Loin

Brining in a blend of kosher salt, sugar, and spices infuses this pork with wonderful flavor and keeps it tender and juicy. Allow the pork to soak in the brine for 18-24 hours before roasting.

Prep:	20 minutes
Marinating:	18-24 hours
Roast:	about 1 hour

1/4 cup	sugar
1/4 cup	kosher salt
2 tbsp.	coriander seeds
2 tbsp.	cracked black pepper
2 tbsp.	fennel seeds
2 tbsp.	cumin seeds
1 peel	from navel orange, with pith removed
1	boneless pork loin roast (about 3 pounds) trimmed
4	garlic cloves, crushed with side of chef's knife

In a 2-quart saucepan, heat 1 cup water with sugar, salt, coriander, pepper, fennel, cumin, and orange peel to boiling over high heat. Reduce heat to low; simmer 2 minutes. Remove saucepan from heat; stir in 3 cups ice until almost melted. Stir in 1 cup cold water.

Place pork in large self-sealing plastic bag with garlic and brine. Seal bag, pressing out excess air. Place bag in bowl or small roasting pan and refrigerate for 18-24 hours.

When ready to cook, preheat oven to 400 degrees. Remove pork from bag; discard the brine (it's OK if some spices stick to the pork). Place pork on rack in small roasting pan (14" by 10"). Insert meat thermometer into thickest part of pork. Roast about 1 hour to 1 hour 15 minutes or until thermometer reaches 150 degrees (temperature will rise 5 degrees to 10 degrees upon standing). Transfer pork to cutting board and let stand 10 minutes to allow juices to set for easier slicing.

Note: Pork loin was split into 3 smaller pieces so as to be sliced for finger sandwiches. This impacted the cooking time to less than suggested time above.

Makes 12 main-dish servings. ❀

⏶ GARY AND CHUCKIE

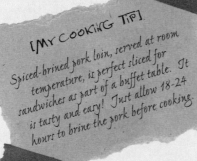

[MY COOKING TIP]

Spiced-brined pork loin, served at room temperature, is perfect sliced for sandwiches as part of a buffet table. It is tasty and easy! Just allow 18-24 hours to brine the pork before cooking.

Visits to well established gardens in your area can inspire by showing plants, planting combinations, gardening techniques and ornamentation which can be useful when translated back to your own garden.
— Gary

ENTRÉES

115

DEBBIE BOEHM
Flower Show Volunteer

Le Stew

2 1/2 lbs. cubed chuck meat
8 minced shallots
4 ozs. cognac (or sherry)
parsley, chopped
4 cups beef broth

2 good handfuls green beans
6 carrots
4 medium potatoes
6 small onions
the above cut into bite size pieces

1/2 tsp. dry mustard
1 1/2 cups red wine
12 large mushrooms, sliced

Sauté shallots and brown beef. Season with salt and pepper. Add sherry, chopped parsley and beef broth. Cover, cook on stove top for one hour.

While that is cooking, prepare vegetables. Cook beans in salted water. Remove beans, preserve water. Use same water, add more if necessary, and cook carrots. Follow same procedure for onions next. Then potatoes. To the cooking potatoes, add the dry mustard. Save vegetable water.

Add wine to meat; cook 30 more minutes. Add vegetable water (about 1 cup). Simmer covered as long as you like to combine the flavors.

Fifteen minutes before serving, add vegetables and sliced mushrooms. Serve with green salad and crusty bread. The flavor is very rich.

Serves 4-6 ✿

Duck with Green Peppercorn Sauce

I	4 I/2 lb. duck
I/2 tsp.	salt

I/4 cup	shallots, chopped
I cup	whipping cream
3 tbsp.	cognac or brandy
2 tbsp.	drained green peppercorns in brine

Using poultry shears, cut the duck in half lengthwise. Cut along both sides of back bone and remove back bone. Cut through breast bone. Cut each half into 2 pieces so you have 2 leg/thigh and 2 breast /wing pieces.

Heat a large skillet. Add the duck pieces, skin side down, sprinkle with salt and cool over high heat for 5 minutes. Lift the pieces so they don't stick. Leave skin side down.

Reduce heat to low and cover tightly. Cook until the duck skin is very brown, about I5 minutes. Turn heat to very low, cover and cook until the duck is tender, about 30 minutes.

Remove duck from skillet to a platter and keep warm in a low oven.

Pour most of the rendered duck fat into a small bowl. Using a small amount (I-2 tablespoons) of the fat, sauté the shallots.

Add whipping cream, cognac and peppercorns. Boil mixture until it thickens to a sauce consistency, about 6 minutes. Season to taste with pepper. Serve with duck.

Note: If you like crisper duck skin, place the pieces in a preheated broiler, skin side up, for a few minutes.

Serves 2-4 ❊

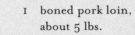

JODY HAWKINS

Marinated Pork Loin

I	boned pork loin, about 5 lbs.
I 1/4 cups	dry red wine
I cup	olive oil
3	cloves garlic, chopped
3	juniper berries, crushed
2 tsp.	dried rosemary or 2 or 3 tablespoons fresh rosemary
1/2 tsp.	dried thyme
I tsp.	salt
1/2 tsp.	pepper

Combine wine, garlic, juniper berries, rosemary, thyme, olive oil, salt and pepper. Add pork loin and marinate in refrigerator for 6 – 8 hours, turning often. Can be placed in a zip lock plastic bag and rotated frequently.

Place loin on a rack in a roasting pan and roast uncovered for I 3/4 to 2 hours or until meat thermometer reads 155 degrees to 160 degrees. Remove roast to cutting board and let stand for 15 minutes. Carve and place meat on serving platter, serve with sauce.

Serves 8-10 ❧

SAUCE:

2 tbsp.	oil
1/2 cup	red wine
I cup	chicken broth
3	finely chopped shallots
3 tbsp.	cornstarch dissolved in 3 tbsp. water
1/2 cup	half and half

Put roasting pan with juices over low to medium heat. Add wine, broth and any juices from carving. Boil for approximately I minute. Reduce heat and add cornstarch mixture. Stir until thickened. Add half and half. (Can be left out.) ❧

ENTRÉES

Beef Brisket

Sear meat under the broiler, one side at a time. Season with minced garlic; Lawry's Seasoning Salt. Add 3-4 bay leaves into the crevices of the meat.

MAKES A GREAT SANDWICH! Can be made for sandwiches by placing on French or Italian rolls with sautéed onions and mushrooms.

Place into a baking pan with a very tight lid. Quarter 2 large Vidalia onions and add to the baking pan, along with 1/4 cup water.

Bake at 350 degrees for 2 1/2 hours, basting every 1/2 hour.

Cool completely on counter. When completely cool, refrigerate.

The following day, SLICE AGAINST THE GRAIN, and re-heat at 325 degrees with a tight lid for 1/2 hour. ❧

◀ STAN WITH WIFE, SUSAN

CHUCK MARTIN
Food Editor, Cincinnati Enquirer

Baked Penne with Spring Vegetables

I lb.	fresh spinach, washed and tough stems removed
I tbsp.	olive oil
	salt and pepper, to taste
I lb.	cremini or other mushrooms, cleaned and cut into thick slices
3 tbsp.	butter, divided
I lb.	asparagus, tough ends removed and cut into I-inch pieces
2 cups	heavy cream
I tsp.	minced lemon zest
I	garlic clove, finely minced
1/8 tsp.	red pepper flakes (optional)
I cup	grated Parmesan
I cup	shredded fontina
I cup	ricotta
I tsp.	salt
I lb.	penne or other tubular pasta

A garden always gives back more than it receives.
— Mara Beamish

Add olive oil to large pan over medium high heat and wilt spinach quickly, stirring often. Add salt and pepper to taste and drain briefly in colander. Squeeze excess moisture from spinach and chop coarsely. Set aside.

Sauté sliced mushrooms in 1 tablespoon butter over medium high heat until moisture in pan evaporates. Add salt and pepper to taste and set aside. Melt remaining 2 tablespoons butter and toss with cut asparagus. Set aside.

In large bowl, mix cream with zest, garlic, red pepper, Parmesan, fontina, ricotta and teaspoon salt. Add black pepper to taste and mix well. Set aside.

Bring large pot of water to rapid boil and add generous amount of salt. Add penne, return to boil and cook 4 minutes. Drain pasta briefly, and while still hot, add to cream mixture along with asparagus, mushrooms and spinach. Mix well.

Preheat oven to 500 degrees for 10 minutes. Spray large shallow casserole with vegetable oil spray and turn pasta-cream mixture into dish, spreading it evenly. Place on center rack of oven and bake 16 to 20 minutes, until tips of penne begin to crisp and turn brown. Makes 6 to 8 appetizer servings or 4 main-course servings.

Adapted from Cucina Simpatica (HarperCollins). ❧

Ice Cream Cone Flowers
SPONSOR: HYDE PARK SQUARE,
ARTIST: CARRIE LYNN COOKE

American Beauty
SPONSOR: AMERICAN AIRLINES
EMPLOYEES, ARTIST:
JULIE SCHULTZ

Land & Sea
SPONSOR: ANONYMOUS,
ARTIST: LISA WALLE

ENTRÉES

CHUCK SCHRAMM
Flower Show Volunteer, and 2000 Volunteer of the Year

Braised Pork Chops in Bourbon and Thyme

4	each center cut pork chops — with fat removed
1	medium onion
1 cup	Bourbon Whiskey
1-1/2 tbsp.	dried thyme
	salt and pepper
1/2 cup	water

Place a small amount of good oil in a heavy skillet. (Skillet and lid should be oven proof.) Pat the surfaces of the pork chops dry, so they will brown nicely. Salt and pepper. Dust with flour. Brown in hot oil. After the pork chops are browned, drain all of the oil from the skillet.

Goes well with buttered French cut green beans and mashed garlic potatoes. Enjoy!
– Chuck

Thinly slice the onion and place in the hot skillet. Turn heat to high and quickly sauté, brown but do not burn the onions. After the onions are finished, spread them evenly over the bottom of the skillet and then place the pork chops on top. Apply another application of black pepper if you like.

Pour the Bourbon Whiskey and water over the meat. Sprinkle the dried thyme over the tops of the pork chops. The liquid should just about cover the meat. Cover.

Place in a 325 degree oven for approximately one hour or until tender. Check after 30 minutes to be sure skillet still contains adequate liquid. When finished remove from oven. Remove the pork chops from the remaining liquid and keep them warm.

GRAVY:

Place the skillet with the remaining liquid on burner and bring to simmer. Place one tablespoon corn starch in small dish with approximately 1/4 cup milk. Depending on how much liquid remains from the braising, it may take more milk and corn starch. The amount above is for about 1 1/2 cups liquid. Also if you want your gravy thicker you may add more corn starch. Add more salt and pepper to taste.

Serves 2 ❁

SHERIE MAREK
Domestic Goddess and Community Volunteer

Beef Burgundy

3	onions cut into 1/8's and sliced
1 cup	carrot slices
8 sprigs	parsley (no stems)
1/3 cup	flour
2 1/2 tsp.	salt
1/2 tsp.	garlic salt
1/4 tsp.	pepper
3 lbs.	beef filet
1/4 cup	olive oil
1/3 cup	cognac
4 slices	bacon, cut in small pieces
1/2 tsp.	thyme
1	bay leaf
1 cup	Burgundy
1/2 lb.	fresh mushrooms sliced and sautéed

Chop onions coarse. Dry chop carrots and parsley. Reserve.

Combine next 4 ingredients. Mix. Dredge meat in flour mixture. Heat olive oil in large Dutch oven. Add meat. Brown well. Sprinkle remaining flour mix. Pour cognac, flame. Cook bacon and chopped vegetables until bacon browns. Stir in thyme, pour over meat. Add bay leaf and pour wine mixture.

[COMMENT ON FLOWER POWER]
The color and design of the Flower Power pots brought freshness to the Queen City — Thanks to CHS!

Cook 325 degrees for one hour. Add mushrooms.

Serves 6-8. ✽

QUOTE ON GARDENING
Gardens are like fingerprints- unique- choose what makes you happy.

ERNEST L. ROBINSON
CHS Board Member/Exhibitor

Eggplant Festival

1	medium eggplant, pared and cut into thin strips
2 - 2 1/2 cups	cooked chicken or turkey, cut into thin strips
1/4 cup	thinly sliced green peppers
1/4 cup	thinly sliced red bell peppers
1/4 cup	thinly sliced orange bell peppers
1/4 cup	thinly sliced red onions
1/4 cup	thinly sliced mushrooms
1 tbsp.	dried oregano
1/2 tsp.	thyme
1 tbsp.	paprika
1/2 tsp.	cinnamon
1/2 cup	virgin olive oil
1/2 cup	white wine

Place eggplant in mixing bowl. Add prepared ingredients and spices. Toss gently. Add chicken or turkey, mix gently.

Place entire mixture in baking dish. Drizzle olive oil and wine over entire mixture. Cover and bake in oven at 350 degrees. Cook for one hour.

Check dish after 45 minutes to ensure that dish does not over cook. Serve over rice or pasta.

Serves 6 ❋

LAURA PULFER

Author and Cincinnati Enquirer Columnist

Lamb Shanks in Red Wine

St. George and the Snap Dragon
SPONSOR: MARGE AND JIM ANDERSON, ARTIST: BJ SIMPSON

6	lamb shanks
	salt and pepper
	flour
1	large onion, minced
1	clove garlic, minced
2 cups	dry red wine
4 stalks	celery, finely chopped
1	bay leaf
1/2 tsp.	thyme

Salt and pepper lamb, dust with flour. Brown shanks in butter or olive oil. Add onion and garlic. Cook until onion is soft. Pour wine over shanks, add celery, carrots and herbs. Cover, bake at 350 degrees for 1 1/2 to 2 hours or until lamb is tender. Add more wine or water if needed during baking. ✱

Fern Gully
SPONSOR: AUXILARY OF BETHESDA HOSPITAL, ARTIST: BJ SIMPSON

▲ MARY MARGARET ROCHFORD AND LAURA

The Flower Trip
SPONSOR: CINCINNATI FLOWER SHOW, ARTIST: MAEVE ROCHFORD SCHULZ

ENTRÉES

125

KAY GREIWE
Flower Show Volunteer

Crab Mornay Florentine

3 packages chopped spinach
1 clove chopped garlic
2 tbsp. grated onion
6 tbsp. butter
4 tbsp. flour
3 cups milk
1 cup grated Swiss cheese
1 cup milk
2 tsp. lemon juice
pinch of garlic salt
dash of nutmeg
salt and cayenne to taste
2 lbs. crabmeat
1 cup fresh bread crumbs

Cook spinach with garlic and onions. Drain. Transfer to 2 quart baking dish or 8 oven proof shells. Melt butter and add flour. Gradually add milk. Add cheese and 1 cup milk and seasonings. Cook over low heat until thick — about 10 minutes. Fold in crab. Pour mixture over spinach and top with bread crumbs. May be made ahead. Bake 350 degrees for 30 minutes til bubbly.

Serves 8 ❀

▲ BOB AND KAY GREIWE

126

Joyce

JOYCE RE
CHS Volunteer

Mama Mia Lasagne

2 lb. ground turkey
2 large cans Contadina tomato paste
1 large jar Prego sauce (onion/garlic)
3 onions
2 peppers
  onion salt, garlic salt - Mrs. Dash, minced onions, black pepper and oregano to taste
3 jars sliced mushrooms (or fresh and sliced)
1 large container small curd cottage cheese or ricotta cheese
3 packages shredded mozzarella cheese
  grated Parmesan cheese
2 eggs
1 box lasagne noodles

I don't follow a book — just estimate! Slice and serve with salad, bread sticks and polenta. Enjoy! — Joyce

Preheat over to 350 degrees.

Brown turkey and place in large pot (or crock-pot). Add Contadina and dilute with water. Add Prego sauce. Add 2 chopped onions, chopped peppers and mushrooms. Add seasoning to taste. Slow cook for 5-7 hours. Add one whole onion during cooking process. When finished cooking, remove onion.

Cook noodles per package directions. When cooked, rinse with cold water and leave in pot to prevent pasta from sticking together. Mix eggs and ricotta or cottage cheese and set aside. Spray large baking dish with non-stick spray. Cover bottom of dish with layer of sauce; add one layer of lasagne; add small amount of eggs and cottage cheese mix. Spread with layer of mozzarella. Sprinkle with Parmesan. Continue layering until dish is full.

Cover with foil and bake for 40 minutes. Uncover and continue baking for 20 minutes or until browned and bubbly. Remove from oven and set aside for 10 minutes to firm.

Serves 10. ✿

SISTER FRANCIS MARIE THRAILKILL
President, College of Mount St. Joseph

Chicken and Seafood Jambalaya

SEASONING MIX:

2	whole bay leaves		I cup	chopped celery
I 1/2 tsp.	salt		1/4 cup	chopped green bell peppers
I 1/2 tsp.	ground red pepper (preferably cayenne)		1/2 cup	chicken, cut in bite-size pieces (about 3 ounces)
I 1/2 tsp.	dried oregano leaves		I 1/2 tsp.	minced garlic
I 1/4 tsp.	white pepper		3	medium size tomatoes, peeled, chopped (about I lb.)
I tsp.	black pepper			
3/4 tsp.	dried thyme leaves		3/4 cup	canned tomato sauce
2 1/2 tbsp.	lard or bacon fat		2 cups	basic seafood stock (or you can use chicken stock)
2/3 cup	chopped tasso (smoked ham-about 3 ounces)			
1/2 cup	chopped andouille smoked sausage...about 3 ounces – (in a pinch you could use kielbasa)		1/2 cup	chopped green onions
			2 cups	uncooked rice (converted not instant)
			I 1/2 dozen	peeled medium shrimp (about 1/2 lb.)
I 1/2 cups	chopped onions			

Optional—1 1/4 dozen oysters in their liquid (about 10 ounces)

Combine the seasoning mix in a small bowl and set aside. In a 4-quart saucepan, melt the fat over medium heat...add the tasso and andouille and sauté until crisp...about 5-7 minutes, stirring frequently. Add onions, celery and bell peppers...sauté until tender, but still firm (about 5 minutes), stirring occasionally and scraping pan bottom. Add the chicken, raise the heat to high and cook I minute, stirring constantly. Reduce heat to medium; add the seasonings and minced garlic. Cook about 3 minutes, stirring constantly and scraping pan bottom as needed. Add the tomatoes and cook until the chicken is tender (about 5-8 minutes) stirring frequently. Add the tomato sauce; cook about 7 minutes stirring fairly often. Stir in the stock and bring to a boil. Stir in the green onions and cook about 2 minutes stirring once or twice. Add the rice, shrimp and oysters, stir well and remove from heat.

Transfer to an ungreased 8 by 8 inch baking pan...cover pan snugly (the rice has to steam so don't neglect this direction) bake at about 350 degrees until rice is tender but still a bit crunchy....NOT clumpy or stuck together...about 30 minutes. Remove bay leaves and serve immediately. ✽

If you want more spice...
serve the Creole sauce.

CREOLE SAUCE
SEASONING MIX:

2	bay leaves
3/4 tsp.	dried oregano
1/2 tsp.	salt
1/2 tsp.	white pepper
1/2 tsp.	black pepper
1/2 tsp.	sweet paprika
1/2 tsp.	red pepper
1/2 tsp.	dried thyme
1/2 tsp.	dried sweet basil leaves
3 tbsp.	unsalted butter
1 cup	peeled and chopped tomatoes
1/4 cup	chopped onions
3/4 cup	chopped celery
1/4 cup	chopped green peppers
1 1/2 tsp.	minced garlic
1 1/4 cups	basic chicken stock
1 cup	canned tomato sauce
1 tsp.	sugar

Thoroughly combine the seasoning mix...set aside. Melt the butter in a
large skillet over medium heat...stir in tomatoes, onions, celery and bell
peppers...then add seasoning mix and garlic...stir thoroughly. Sauté until
onions are transparent, (about 5 minutes) stirring occasionally. Stir in
stock, tomato sauce, sugar and Tabasco...bring to a boil but reduce heat
immediately to maintain a simmer...cook until vegetables are tender and the
flavors are married...about 20 minutes. Remove bay leaves and serve over
Jambalaya or any dish you want to "spice up"...even omelets. ✿

STEPHEN BENNETT

Director of Shows, The Royal Horticultural
Society and CHS Advisor

Suprême de Volaille au Kari (Breast of chicken with curry sauce)

2 tbsp.   butter
3 tbsp.   flour
1 tbsp.   curry powder
1 1/2 cups rich chicken broth (see
           recipe for poached
           chicken)
1/2 cup   heavy cream
1/4 cup   chopped chutney
2   whole poached chicken
           breasts (see recipe)

Melt the butter in a saucepan and
add the flour and curry powder,
stirring with a wire whisk. When
blended and smooth, add the
broth, stirring constantly. Add the
cream and the chutney and bring to
the simmer.

Remove the skin and bones from
the chicken. Carefully remove the
breast halves, each in one piece.
Arrange one breast half on each of
four hot plates. Spoon equal portions of the sauce over each breast
half. Serve with plain rice or rice
with raisins and coconut.

Serves 4

A Pierre Franey recipe. ❀

SUPRÊME DE VOLAILLE POCHÉ
(POACHED BREAST OF CHICKEN)

2   large, whole chicken
           breasts, about 2 lbs.
1 cup   fresh or canned chicken broth
           water to cover
1/2 cup   coarsely chopped celery
1/2 cup   coarsely chopped onion
1/2 tsp.   dried thyme
1   bay leaf
           salt to taste
12   peppercorns
1   sprig fresh parsley
1/2 cup   coarsely chopped carrot

Put chicken breasts in one layer in a
saucepan. Add the broth and water to
cover. Add remaining ingredients,
cover, bring to a boil and simmer
about 10 minutes. ❀

SUE DVORAK
CHS Publicity Manager

Chicken Saltimbocca

4	boneless, skinless chicken breasts
1	large bunch of fresh sage leaves (appx. 36 leaves)
4	thin slices of prosciutto
4 tbsp.	olive oil
1/4 cup	flour
1/4 cup	dry white wine
1/4 cup	Marsala or Port wine
3/4 cup	chicken broth
1 tbsp.	chopped sage
	freshly ground black pepper and salt to taste
4	slices Fontina cheese

Pound chicken between sheets of wax paper to 1/4" thickness; place about 6 large sage leaves on half of the face of the pounded chicken breast, cover sage leaves with a prosciutto slice and then a slice of Fontina and fold over other half of chicken and secure with a toothpick. Chill in refrigerator for 10 minutes. Place half of the oil in large heavy skillet and heat over medium high heat; dredge two of the chicken breasts in flour and sauté chicken until cooked through — about 2-3 minutes on each side; repeat with remaining oil and remaining chicken breasts; remove from chicken pan, cover and keep warm.

Add white wine and Marsala or Port to skillet and boil, scraping up brown bits; add chicken stock and boil until reduced. Add chopped sage and simmer about 1 minute. Add pepper and salt to taste; pour over chicken and serve immediately.

Serves: 4 ❀

JEFF AND MICHELLE WEECH
Friends of the Flower Show

Chicken Fajitas

1 lb.	boneless chicken breast
6 to 8	flour tortillas
	onion and bell pepper cut
	into long, thin strips
	oil (peanut or corn)
	salsa
	mild cheddar cheese, grated

MARINADE FOR CHICKEN:

3 tbsp.	lime juice
3 tbsp.	olive oil
1	clove garlic, crushed
1 to 2 tsp.	chili powder
1/2 tsp.	sugar
1/4 tsp.	salt
1/4 tsp.	black pepper

Mix the marinade and add chicken. Refrigerate for 6 to 24 hours.

Grill the chicken and cut into 1/2" slices.

Over medium high heat, in a dry (no oil) skillet, toast the tortillas individually for about 20 to 30 seconds on each side. Place in a folded-over piece of foil to stay warm (do not place into the oven.) They should still be soft, not crispy. Now add the sliced onion and bell peppers and sprinkle with oil. Sauté for a few minutes until the vegetables are slightly browned. Remove from heat.

Build a fajita with several chunks of chicken, onion and bell peppers, salsa and cheddar cheese.

FRESH SALSA:

3	vine ripened tomatoes
1	cucumber
2 tbsp.	onion
1	jalapeno pepper
1 tbsp.	vinegar
	salt and pepper to taste

Authentic Tex-Mex style dinner is served with Spanish rice and refried beans. A great way to use your garden fresh vegetables. Make salsa from scratch with your favorite recipe.

Dice tomatoes into 1/2 inch pieces, drain and add to bowl. Peel and dice cucumber hull (remove seed section) and add to bowl. Add finely diced onion and jalapeno to taste. Add salt and allow to 'sweat' for 10 minutes; drain. Add pepper and vinegar and mix gently. Chill until ready to serve. ❁

GIL RICHARDS
Friend of CHS

Mrs. Richards' Pasta with Roasted Tomatoes

▲ GIL WITH MARSHA HABERER

5	ripe tomatoes, good size (do not use plum tomatoes — they get dried out)
1/2 cup	olive oil
8	cloves of garlic
1 tbsp.	kosher salt
1 tbsp.	pepper
	handful of fresh basil, chopped
1 cup	fresh Parmesan cheese
	pasta

Core tomatoes and slice in half. Lay in baking dish. If dish isn't big enough, just pile on top of each other. Chop garlic and top generously on tomatoes. Sprinkle tomatoes with kosher salt, pepper. Pour olive oil over tomatoes.

Bake for 2 hours at 350 degrees. When pasta is ready, take tomatoes out of oven. With two knives, break up tomatoes, add to pasta. Add chopped basil and Parmesan cheese.

Serve with salad and bread.

Serves 4 ❧

It's difficult to think anything
but pleasant thoughts while eating
a homegrown tomato.
— Lewis Grizzard

I don't know whether nice people

tend to grow roses

or growing roses makes people nice.

— ROLAND A BEOWNE

Impatiens are a Virtue ▶

SPONSOR: LOIS AND DICK ROSENTHAL, ARTIST: SARAH JANE BELLAMY

SANDWICHES, SIDES & SAVORY FARE

BARBARA HILDEBRANDT

CHS Development Director

Mary Duke's Sweet Potato Casserole

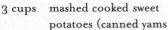

3 cups	mashed cooked sweet potatoes (canned yams will also work)
1 cup	sugar
1/2 cup	melted butter
2 eggs	well beaten
1 tsp.	vanilla extract
1/3 cup	milk

Combine ingredients and mix well. Spoon into a 2 quart casserole and bake for 35 min. at 350.

This is a family recipe from Johnson City, TN. It makes an excellent dish to serve at Thanksgiving and is easy especially if you use canned yams. Enjoy!
– Barb

TOPPING (OPTIONAL):

1/2 cup	firmly packed brown sugar
1/4 cup	all purpose flour
2 1/2 tbsp.	melted butter
1/2 cup	chopped pecans

Sprinkle on top of casserole before baking. *

English Garden Party Sandwiches

9 ozs.	soft fresh goat cheese
1/2 cup	chopped watercress
1 tsp.	truffle oil (Sur La Table has)
12	very thin slices white bread
1	bunch radishes, very thinly sliced
1/2	English Hot House cucumber, peeled and thinly sliced

[Quote on Cooking]
During the warm months, cook dinners that can be eaten in the garden. Try these Tea Sandwiches sitting by the roses.

Blend goat cheese, watercress and truffle oil in processor until just combined. Season with salt and pepper.

Place bread slices on work surface. Spread each with goat cheese mixture, dividing equally. Set aside 24 radishes for garnish.

Top 6 bread slices with cucumber slices, then remaining radish slices. Sprinkle with pepper. Top with remaining bread slices, cheese side down. (Can be made 2 hours ahead.)

Wrap individually in paper towels, chill. Trim sandwich crusts. Cut each sandwich into 4 squares. Transfer to sandwich platter. Top each with 1 radish, slice and serve.

Makes 24 sandwiches ❧

*How can anyone remain angry
when looking at flowers? – Cindi and David*

Grilled Vegetables on Flour Tortillas

2	zucchini, cut into 1/2" slices
2	yellow squash, cut into 1/2" slices
4	tomatoes, cut into chunks
1	red or yellow bell pepper, cut into 1" pieces
1	large red or Vidalia onion, cut into 1" pieces
1/2 cup	cilantro, chopped
3 tbsp.	olive oil
1 tbsp.	ground cumin
	salt & pepper to taste
	flour tortillas
	sour cream
	guacamole (optional)
	salsa
	cheddar cheese

Laughter is the brightest in the place where the food is.
- Irish proverb

Toss all ingredients together in bowl (it may look like a lot, but when they cook, they shrink considerably) and let sit for at least one hour. Heat grill, place vegetables in veggie tray. Grill over hot coals until tender and browned. Serve with flour tortillas, sour cream, guacamole, cheddar cheese and salsa.

This is a great recipe year-round and can be made ahead of time. Although, when the produce comes right from your garden, it always tastes better. You can add some mesquite chips to the grill, it takes on a new flavor.

Serves 4-6 ✿

JUDY MITCHELL
CHS Board Member

Fresh Spinach Sauté

1-2 tbsp.   butter
dash of olive oil
minced garlic (I tsp. or to taste)
2 tbsp.   soy sauce
fresh spinach

Add butter, olive oil and garlic to 8" skillet. Simmer until blended then add spinach. Cover and cook until tender. ✳

Salsa Bouquet
SPONSOR: CINCINNATUS ASSOCIATION,
ARTIST: MARYANNE COWGILL

Forget-Me-Nots
SPONSOR: EDENVIEW ADULT DAY SERVICES CENTER,
ARTISTS: EDENVIEW ARTISTS

🔺 JUDY AND FRIENDS

The only thing more fun than growing plants is eating them.
— Judy

Geometrics & Flowers
SPONSOR: KAREN AND LOU FRIEDMAN, ARTIST:
KAREN RAE FRIEDMAN

SANDWICHES, SIDES & SAVORY FARE

139

Chicken and Asparagus Sandwich

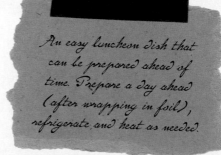

2 cups	cooked chicken, diced
1/3 cup	mayonnaise
1/4 cup	celery, diced
	salt and pepper to taste
8	slices bread
1/2 cup	butter
1	package seasoned coating mix for chicken (Shake & Bake)
8	asparagus — fresh or frozen

An easy luncheon dish that can be prepared ahead of time. Prepare a day ahead (after wrapping in foil), refrigerate and heat as needed.

Heat oven to 400 degrees.

Combine chicken, mayonnaise and celery. Spread on 4 slices of bread. Arrange asparagus spears on top of filling (two for each slice) and top with remaining bread. Melt butter: brush on both sides of sandwiches. Coat sandwiches with seasoned mix and brown on both sides in a buttered skillet. Wrap in foil. Bake in oven approximately 20 minutes or until heated through.

Serves 4 ✤

MARY SCHUMACHER
SVP, Coney Island Park

Beef Barbeque

3 lbs.	cubed chuck roast
2 tbsp.	vegetable oil
3	medium yellow onions
2 tbsp.	cider vinegar
1 tbsp.	brown sugar
1 cup	water
1 tbsp.	lemon juice
1 cup	ketchup - preferably Brooks Spicy Ketchup
1 cup	diced celery
2 tsp.	salt
3 tbsp.	Worcestershire sauce (Lea & Perrins)

Heat oil lightly in dutch oven. Add meat and onions and cook until browned. Lower heat and add remaining ingredients. Stir to mix. Bake in oven at 325 degrees covered until meat is tender/falling apart (approx. 3-4 hours). Mash with a potato masher and serve.

Check barbeque while baking. Add more water if needed.

Serve with your favorite cheese potatoes and cole slaw. YUM! ❧

This recipe has been in our family for over 50 years! I know my grandmother served this, so it most probably dates a generation or two earlier. It's a great recipe for a casual party....... can be made in advance and reheated.
P.S. True barbeque lovers always add a spoonful of home made cole slaw to their sandwich!
– Mary

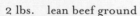

NADINE BRUNNER
Volunteer and small business owner

Mrs. Bohmer's Sloppy Joes

2 lbs.	lean beef ground
2 tbsp.	Crisco
2	large onions, chopped
4 tbsp.	sugar
1 tsp.	prepared mustard
2 tbsp.	vinegar
2 tsp.	salt
2	14 ounce bottles of catsup (Brooks Tangy)

Cook beef and onions slowly in Crisco. Add remaining ingredients and simmer about 45 minutes or one hour.

For best results, use exact measurements. ❧

▲ NADINE WITH DAUGHTER, MEGGAN

Studying with a Belgian Chef while overseas taught me to have everything chopped readied and prepped before beginning.

Author, *Joy of Cooking* and Flower and Farm Fest Guest Chef

Buffalo Burgers

1 lb.	ground buffalo
1/2	sweet onion, diced
1 tbsp.	soy sauce
1 tsp.	hot red pepper sauce
Generous grinding black pepper	

Mix in a large bowl. Form into patties. Let sit to allow flavors to marry for 2 minutes to 2 hours. If preparing more than 15 minutes ahead of time, let patties sit in the refrigerator. Grill until desired degree of doneness. Buffalo is best cooked medium rare to medium.

Ethan Becker recently created this recipe, made from ground buffalo of Vista Grand Ranch, New Richmond, Ohio.

Makes 4 - 4 ounce patties. ✽

Cooking is always enriched by ingredients you grow in your own garden. There's nothing like walking into the kitchen with a warm, ripe tomato and a handful of fragrant basil. Yum.

— Ethan

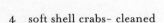

KEVIN O'DELL - Exhibitor and CHS Board Member
SARAH MILLER - 2002 Volunteer of the Year

Soft Shell Crab Sandwich

4	soft shell crabs- cleaned
1/2 cup	flour
1-2 tbsp.	Old Bay Seasoning
3-4 tbsp.	butter, margarine or oil
4	sandwich buns ripe red tomato-sliced leaf lettuce

Grab a beach chair and enjoy!

To Prepare:

Drive 12 hours to Wancheese, NC and get your fresh soft shells at O'Neals Seafood and stop at a farmers market for lettuce/tomatoes. Drive 2 hours to Hatteras, NC, take ramp #55, put SUV in 4-wheel drive (let air out of tires to 18psi), drive onto beach to designated spot.

Pull out the Coleman stove-fire it up, and place the butter, margarine or oil in skillet. In plastic bag, mix flour and Old Bay Seasoning. Put soft shells in bag and dust. Place in hot skillet, fry 3-4 minutes per side.

While frying, slice tomato, get out some paper plates and fix yourself one of our favorite beverages (Rum/Ginger Beer – 2 oz. Meyers Dark Rum, 4 oz. Stewarts Ginger Beer, large lime slice and lots of ice).

Place soft shells on bun with sliced tomatoes/lettuce.

*Perona Farms Smoked Salmon & White Cheddar Sandwich Griddled
with Warm Tomato & Tarragon Soup*

SANDWICH:

8 oz.	smoked salmon, sliced
4 oz.	Vermont white cheddar, slices
24 pcs.	bread & butter pickles
1 loaf	Hawaiian Bread
2 tbsp.	butter, soften

Construct sandwiches by layering salmon, cheese & pickles. Lightly butter both sides of bread. Place in a pre-heated panini machine or hot Teflon skillet and brown bread. Cut in any shape you desire.

SOUP:

1 cup	onion
1 tbsp.	butter
2 tbsp.	tomato paste
3 cups	tomato puree
3 cups	chix broth
1 cup	heavy cream
1 oz.	tarragon, freshly chopped

Sauté onion until golden brown. Add tomato products and simmer. Add chix broth and heavy cream. Adjust seasoning. Add tarragon ala minute'.

◄
Sewing Seeds in Cincinnati
SPONSOR: GREATER CINCINNATI
FOUNDATION, ARTIST: KRISTEL KULA

DAVID PEPPER
Cincinnati City Council

Macaroni and Cheese

16 oz.	bags of shredded colby, sharp and mild cheddar, Monterey Jack
1	pkg. (12 slices) real American cheese slices
2	sticks butter
1/8 tsp.	salt
2 cloves	garlic
1/4 slice	of whole red, yellow and green bell peppers

1	16 oz. box macaroni
1	medium size onion
2 cups	vitamin-D milk
1	stalk celery with fresh leaves still on stalk
2	extra large eggs
	Lawry's seasoned salt
	black pepper

Pre-heat oven to 350 degrees. In large cooking pot fill half full with cold water and sprinkle 1/8 tsp. salt. Place on large burner of stove, add 1/2" slice butter and bring to a boil. Add box of macaroni following cooking instructions on box. After draining macaroni in colander rinse with hot water, drain again and pour into roasting pan.

Rinse vegetables in cold water. Chop them all into small squares and place on top of the macaroni. Slice remaining butter and place with vegetables and macaroni in roasting pan. Sprinkle all of the shredded cheeses into pan. Take the American cheese slices out of the wrappers and place them one on top of the other in two stacks of sixes. Then cut the stacked slices into about 1" squares and place into the roasting pan. Now take medium sized bowl and pour in the 2 cups of milk. Crack open the two extra large eggs and add to the milk and with either a fork or the egg whisk or beater, begin mixing them until the egg has completely mixed with the milk and pour into the roasting pan.

Add the Lawry's seasoning salt and pepper to taste. Make sure the macaroni and other ingredients are well saturated with the the milk and egg mixture so that you can see it through your ingredients, if not add more milk.

With large wooden spoon stir, mixing ingredients slightly. Cover with aluminum foil. Place in oven for 40 minutes then remove foil and stir again. Put foil back on and cook about 20-25 minutes. Romove foil and let cook uncovered for about 10 minutes until golden brown. Remove from oven, allow to set for at least 25 minutes. Serve, makes about 25 servings. May make smaller or larger using lesser or greater amounts of ingredients as needed. ❧

Caribbean Woman
SPONSOR: AAA CINCINNATI,
ARTIST: SUSAN SIEGMAN

The Power of Flowers
SPONSOR: URBAN
THICKETS LANDSCAPES,
ARTIST: VANESSA HOLT

Strategic Planting
SPONSOR: ROUGH
BROTHERS, INC.,
ARTIST: EMERSON QUILLIN   147

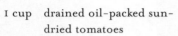

BRUCE RICHARDSON

Owner, Elmwood Inn, Author and Friend of CHS

Sun-dried Tomato Tea Sandwich

SANDWICHES, SIDES & SAVORY FARE

I cup	drained oil-packed sun-dried tomatoes
I	jar (12 oz.) roasted sweet red peppers, drained
I cup	packed fresh basil leaves
1/2 cup	pine nuts, toasted
I tbsp.	olive oil
I tbsp.	balsamic vinegar
2	large garlic cloves
I 1/2 tsp.	grated lemon peel
I	loaf rye or black olive bread

Chop all ingredients in a food processor to make a coarse paste. Season with salt and pepper. Spread on slice of bread. Top with another slice. Trim all edges, then slice diagonally twice, making four triangle sandwiches. ❁

The act of sharing tea with friends in a serene setting surrounded by beautiful art, fresh flowers, delightful foods and great music takes on a spiritual significance not unlike entering a cathedral. This respite brings about a sense of enchantment that people long for in our face-paced society. Tea time urges us to pause, drink deeply, and savor all that is right about the world.

– Bruce

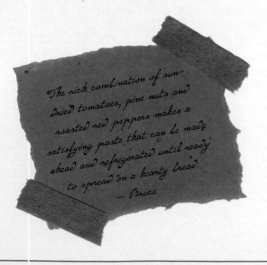

The rich combination of sun-dried tomatoes, pine nuts and roasted red peppers makes a satisfying paste that can be made ahead and refrigerated until ready to spread on a hearty bread.

– Bruce

Olive & Artichoke Tapenade

1 can chopped & drained artichoke hearts (use the kind that doesn't come packed in oil or a marinade)

1 cup chopped olives (combination of black & green or just green)

1 tsp. rosemary

1 tsp. crushed red pepper flakes

3/4 cup olive oil

1/2 cup shredded Parmesan cheese

1/2 cup crumbled feta cheese

1 tbsp. minced garlic

a few capers

salt & pepper to taste at the end

Combine all ingredients in a bowl and mix, let sit in refrigerator for about an hour. Serve with crostini or crackers. ✿

Life's a Beach and Then You Sigh
SPONSOR: HENKLE SCHUELER & ASSOCIATES, INC.,
ARTIST: DEBBIE BURGESS

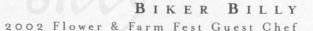

Eggplant Exhaust Pipes

SANDWICHES, SIDES & SAVORY FARE

FOR THE EGGPLANT:

I tbsp.	dried basil
I tsp.	dried oregano
I tsp.	sweet paprika
I tbsp.	onion powder
I tbsp.	garlic powder
I tsp.	black pepper
1/2 tsp.	red pepper flakes
I cup	boiling water
I cup	extra virgin olive oil
I	medium-size eggplant, cut lengthwise into 1/4-inch - thick slices

FOR THE FILLING:

I 1/8 cups	ricotta cheese
1/2 cup	freshly grated Parmesan cheese
1/2 cup	shredded mozzarella cheese
1/2 tsp.	dried basil
1/2 tsp.	dried oregano
1/2 tsp.	salt
1/2 tsp.	black pepper
	After-Burner pasta sauce (recipe follows)
	shredded mozzarella cheese

FOR THE EGGPLANT:

In a small heat proof bowl, combine the basil, oregano, paprika, onion powder, garlic powder, black pepper, red pepper flakes and boiling water; stir well, and allow to cool to room temperature. Add the olive oil and stir well. Brush the mixture on both sides of the eggplant slices, then grill them until tender and browned — three to five minutes per side. Brush them with the flavored oil each time you turn them. Remove from the grill and allow to cool to room temperature.

In a medium-size mixing bowl, combine the filling ingredients, stirring well to blend in the spices.

Preheat the oven to 350 degrees. Cover the bottom of a large baking dish with a layer of pasta sauce. Take a slice of grilled eggplant, place a spoonful of filling at one end, roll the eggplant around it and place in the baking dish. Spoon some sauce over each rolled eggplant, then sprinkle mozzarella cheese on top of each. Repeat until all the eggplant slices are rolled. Bake until the mozzarella is golden brown and the sauce is bubbly, 15 to 20 minutes.

From the book "Biker Billy's HOG Wild on a Harley Cookbook", by Bill Hufnagle ©2003. Reprinted with permission from The Harvard Common Press.

Serves 4-8 ❋

These rolls of breaded and fried eggplants are stuffed with a tasty seasoned cheese blend. Enjoy!
— Biker Billy

▲ Marsha Haberer assists Biker Billy

AFTER-BURNER PASTA SAUCE:

1	dried chipotle pepper, stemmed		
1	dried de Arbol pepper, stemmed		
1	dried New Mexico pepper, stemmed and seeded	1	orange bell pepper, seeded and diced
1/2 cup	boiling water	3 tbsp.	chopped garlic
3 tbsp.	extra virgin olive oil	1 tbsp.	minced fresh oregano leaves
1	Burpee Biker Billy jalapeno, minced	1/2 cup	fresh basil leaves, minced
2	medium-size onions, diced	1 tsp.	salt
1 1/2 cups	sliced mushrooms	1 tsp.	freshly ground black pepper
		1	can peeled whole tomatoes (28 oz.), coarsely chopped, with their juices

Place the chipotle, de Arbol and New Mexico peppers in a small bowl and cover with the boiling water. Allow to cool to room temperature. Puree the rehydrated peppers and soaking water in a blender or a food processor equipped with a chopping blade until no large pieces of pepper remain, about 1 minute.

Heat the olive oil in a large skillet over medium heat. Add the jalapeno, onions, and mushrooms, stir well to coat with the oil. Cook, stirring until the onions are golden brown, five to seven minutes. Add the hot pepper puree, bell pepper, garlic, oregano, basil, salt, black pepper, and tomatoes, bring to a boil, reduce the heat to medium-low and simmer until the sauce just thickens, eight – ten minutes. ✽

VIC NOLTING
President, Coney Island Park

Crab Cakes

2	scallions, finely chopped
2	garlic cloves minced
2 tbsp.	butter
2/3 cup	breadcrumbs
1/3 cup	Italian bread crumbs
1/2 cup	Parmigiano-Reggiano, grated
1/3 cup	mayo
1/4 cup	pimento-finely chopped
2	eggs beaten

2 tbsp.	parsley chopped
1 tbsp.	lemon juice
1 tbsp.	Worcestershire Sauce
1/4 tsp.	cayenne
1 tsp.	dry mustard
1+ tsp.	Old Bay Seasoning
2 tbsp.	butter
2 tbsp.	peanut oil
1 lb.	lump crab meat

Sauté scallions and butter — let cool. Mix breadcrumbs and cheese.

In separate bowl, mix sautéed scallions, mayo, pimento, eggs, parsley, lemon juice, Worcestershire, cayenne, dry mustard and Old Bay Seasoning. Stir in 1/3 cup of bread crumbs/cheese mixture. Fold in crab meat. Cover and chill for two hours.

Shape into patties. Coat with remaining breadcrumbs and cheese mixture. Sauté in 2 tablespoons of butter and 2 tablespoons of peanut oil until browned. Drain and serve with Creole Tartar Sauce, lemon wedge. Garnish with chopped parsley.

Makes approximately 8 patties. ❇

CREOLE TARTAR SAUCE:

1/4 cup	scallions, finely chopped
1/4 cup	celery, finely chopped
1/4 cup	parsley, finely chopped
3 tbsp.	tomato paste
2 tbsp.	Dijon mustard
2 tsp.	olive oil
1 tbsp.	white wine vinegar
3/4 tsp.	Tabasco (or to taste)
1/2 tsp.	paprika

Mix ingredients together. Chill for
2 hours.

Pot de Deux
SPONSOR: BOB AND SANDY
HEIMANN, ARTIST: MICHELLE
SCHULER HEIMANN

Patriotic Posies
SPONSOR: KENT F. HOLWADEL,
ARTIST: CINDY HACKNEY

A Garden of Riches
SPONSOR: HUNTINGTON
FINANCIAL ADVISORS,
ARTIST: CHRISTINE BIERI

DIANA MURPHY
Editor-in-Chief, *Country Living Gardener*

Herbed Vegetable Tian

4 medium zucchini

4 medium yellow summer squash

8 paste tomatoes (or small heirloom tomatoes)

4-6 tbsp. extra-virgin olive oil (or to taste)

2 tbsp. white balsamic vinegar

2 sprigs fresh thyme

2 sprigs fresh rosemary

freshly ground black pepper to taste

Heat oven to 350 degrees. Slice zucchini, yellow squash, and tomatoes into 1/4-inch rounds. In a shallow baking dish, place a slice of zucchini, then yellow squash, then tomato; continue arranging the vegetable slices in this alternating pattern in neat rows down the length of the dish until it is filled. Whisk together the olive oil and white balsamic vinegar and drizzle over vegetables. Remove herb leaves from stalks and sprinkle them over the vegetables. Season with freshly ground pepper to taste, and bake for 30 to 40 minutes, until vegetables are tender. ✿

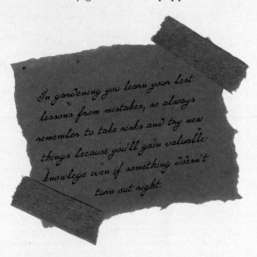

In gardening you learn your best lessons from mistakes, so always remember to take risks and try new things because you'll gain valuable knowlege even if something doesn't turn out right.

This vegetable side dish is super-easy to make, and beautiful enough for an elegant dinner party. It's a great way to use up summer's bounty of herbs and vegetables from your kitchen garden. Serve it with meat, chicken, or fish. For a richer version, tuck in slices of fresh mozzarella or goat cheese. Paste tomatoes, such as 'San Marzano' or 'Principe de Borghese', hold up best for this dish, but I've used small-sized heirloom varieties such as 'Matina', 'Sungold', or 'Brandywine' with great success.

HELEN KOVACH
Volunteer and Friend of CHS

Noodle Ring

3	eggs
3/4 cup	milk (or cream)
1 tbsp.	melted butter
	Salt and pepper to taste
	(I use white pepper)
3 cups	cooked noodles

In a small mixing bowl beat eggs.
Add the milk to eggs. Stir in
melted butter. Season with salt
and pepper.

Butter a medium size ring mold.
Add cooked noodles into mold.
Pour egg mixture over noodles.

Set ring mold into a pan of hot water and bake at 350
degrees for 45 minutes or until a knife inserted into noodles
comes out clean.

Loosen edges with knife and turn noodle ring onto a
warm platter. Fill center with any creamed vegetable or
creamed chicken. ❋

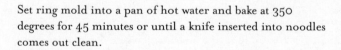

*This dish "wows" guests—and tastes
good too! This is how four generations
in my family "used their noodles."*
— Helen

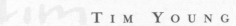

TIM YOUNG

Landscape Designer, Delhi Landscape Services
and 1998 Volunteer of the Year

3 Mushroom & Spinach Omelette

1 dozen	extra large fresh eggs			
1/4 cup	half & half (may substitute 2% milk)			
8 oz.	Swiss cheese wedge or 1/2" slice (cut into 1/2" cubes)			
4 oz.	portabella mushroom	1/2 cup	Vidalia onion-chopped
4 oz.	shitake mushroom	3	lg. cloves of garlic-minced
4 oz.	cremini mushroom	1 oz.	dry white wine
1/2 cup	red bell pepper-chopped	1 oz.	olive oil
1 cup	loose fresh baby spinach-chopped	1	stick butter (or margarine)
		1/2 tsp.	tarragon
		1/2 tbsp.	garlic powder
		1/4 tsp.	black pepper
		1/4 tsp.	salt

Start by combining approximately 1/4 stick butter, wine and olive oil in a large skillet over medium heat. Slice the mushrooms into 1/2" slices and add to skillet. Let sauté approximately 5 minutes, stirring once or twice. Add chopped onions and sauté until clear. Add garlic and sauté for another minute or two. Remove from heat and set aside.

Have in separate bowls the sautéed mushrooms, Swiss cheese, red pepper and spinach. Crack open the eggs into a large bowl and add the half & half, tarragon, garlic powder, black pepper and salt. Whisk this mixture to get a consistent mix.

Preheat a large skillet over medium heat, add some butter — allowing it to melt but not brown, then add approximately 1/4 of egg mixture. Let cook until the eggs start to firm (doesn't take long) and lift the edge to let the top, uncooked egg drain under the cooked egg. After a couple of minutes, when the top is just moist, flip the omelet (this is the tricky part!) I like to slide the omelette into a clean skillet or a large pot lid and flip it back into the skillet. As the omelette is finishing the cooking (approximately 1 minute) add 1/4 of the sautéed mushrooms, Swiss cheese, red pepper and spinach over one half of the omelette surface, then fold over the other half. Slide the omelet onto the serving plate and garnish with a little spinach and red pepper.

Makes approximately 4 omelettes ❁

This is one of my favorites of all the omelettes I make. I like to cube my cheese instead of using shredded and like the mushrooms in thicker slices. This allows you to better savor each ingredient and does not blend the flavors as much.

Every year in the fall I get together with my brother, sister and families. We get up early and go out to a local park to have breakfast. I always cook omelets over an open fire with hashbrowns, biscuits, fresh fruits and bacon. It is always a wonderful day.

This tradition started when I was just starting out in this business and was working at Fort Ancient State Park. My mom and dad would come up every Sunday morning in the fall and dad would make his western omelette for us all.

– Tim

JANE PORTMAN
Community Volunteer

Old-Fashioned Southern Summer Squash Casserole

2 lb.	cooked summer (yellow) squash
I	onion, chopped and sauteed in
1/2	stick butter
I cup	sour cream
3/4 cup	grated sharp cheddar cheese
	salt and pepper to taste
	bread crumbs

Wonderful way to use that bumper crop of squash from your garden!
— Jane

Mash squash and mix with onion, sour cream, cheese, salt and pepper. Top with bread crumbs. Bake 15-20 minutes at 350 degrees. ❧

Count none but sunny hours.
— words attributed to William Hazlitt

PAT HENLEY
Friend of the Flower Show

David Eyre's Pancake

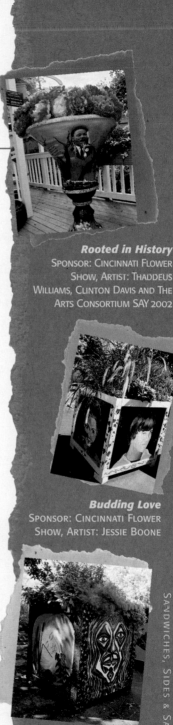

1/2 cup	flour
1/2 cup	milk
2	eggs, lightly beaten
	grated nutmeg
4 tbsp.	butter
2 tbsp.	confectioner's sugar
	juice of half a lemon – or more

Preheat oven to 425. Combine flour, milk, eggs and nutmeg. Beat lightly, but leave batter a little lumpy. Melt butter in 12 inch skillet. Bake 15 to 20 minutes until pancake is golden brown. Sprinkle with sugar and return briefly to oven. Sprinkle with lemon juice and serve immediately. ❀

This recipe, probably collected from Clementine Paddleford's Sunday supplement column years ago, is never fail comfort food for one or two. Serve with a fruit cup and maybe a little Danish pastry for Sunday brunch. But, who was David Eyre?
— Pat

Rooted in History
SPONSOR: CINCINNATI FLOWER SHOW, ARTIST: THADDEUS WILLIAMS, CLINTON DAVIS AND THE ARTS CONSORTIUM SAY 2002

Budding Love
SPONSOR: CINCINNATI FLOWER SHOW, ARTIST: JESSIE BOONE

Vine Street Dreams
SPONSOR: CINCINNATI FLOWER SHOW, ARTIST: LETTIE DAVIS AND ROGER REIFONAS

SANDWICHES, SIDES & SAVORY FARE

159

BRUCE RICHARDSON
Owner, Elmwood Inn, Author and Friend of CHS

Smoked Chicken, Sun-Dried Tomato and Spinach Tea Sandwich

DRESSING:

1/2 cup	oil-packed sun-dried tomatoes, drained and chopped
2 tbsp.	red wine vinegar
2 tbsp.	fresh lemon juice
3/4 cup	olive oil
1/4 cup	chopped shallots
4	grilled or smoked chicken breasts, chopped
1/4 cup	bacon, cooked and crumbled fresh spinach leaves
1	loaf hearty white or wheat bread

In a small bowl, whisk together the red wine vinegar, lemon juice, and olive oil. Add the sun-dried tomatoes and shallots. Set aside.

Place several spinach leaves on top of a piece of bread. Top spinach with chicken mixture, then another piece of bread. Trim crusts, then cut diagonally twice, making four triangles. The sides of the tea sandwich will be colorful with the spinach and tomatoes showing.

Makes about 40 tea sandwiches. 🌸

When you take a flower in your hand and really look at it, it's your world for the moment. I want to give that world to someone else. Most people in the city rush around so, they have no time to look at a flower. I want them to see it whether they want to or not.
- Georgia O'Keeffe

LOG CABIN HERB SOCIETY
Clermont County

Cranberry Biscuit Turkey Sandwiches

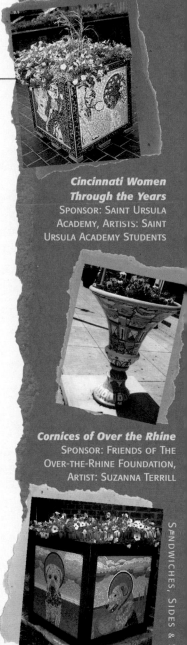

2 tbsp.	cold butter (no substitutes)
4 cups	biscuit/baking mix
I cup	milk
3/4 cup	dried cranberries

CRANBERRY BUTTER:

I/2 cup	butter, softened
I/4 cup	honey
I/4 cup	dried cranberries, chopped
I I/2 lbs.	thinly sliced deli smoked turkey

In a large bowl, cut butter into biscuit mix until crumbly; stir in milk just until moistened. Fold in the cranberries. Turn onto a floured surface; knead IO-I5 times. Roll out to I/2 inch thickness; cut with a 2-I/2 inch biscuit cutter. Place on ungreased baking sheets. Bake at 400 degrees for I4-I6 minutes or until golden brown. Cool on a wire rack.

In a small mixing bowl, beat butter and honey until smooth; stir in cranberries. To assemble sandwiches, split biscuits. Spread with cranberry butter and top with turkey; replace biscuit tops.

Makes 30 sandwiches. 🌿

Cincinnati Women Through the Years
SPONSOR: SAINT URSULA ACADEMY, ARTISTS: SAINT URSULA ACADEMY STUDENTS

Cornices of Over the Rhine
SPONSOR: FRIENDS OF THE OVER-THE-RHINE FOUNDATION, ARTIST: SUZANNA TERRILL

Dogwood Tree Box
SPONSOR: BABIES MILK FUND PEDIATRIC CARE, ARTIST: MATT KOTLARCZYK

SANDWICHES, SIDES & SAVORY FARE

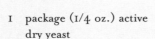

LAURA NOE
CHS Volunteer Coordinator

Chive Pinwheel Rolls

Sandwiches, Sides & Savory Fare

1	package (1/4 oz.) active dry yeast
1/4 cup	warm water (110 degrees to 115 degrees)
1 cup	milk
1/3 cup	vegetable oil
1/4 cup	mashed potatoes (prepared without milk and butter)
1	egg
3 tbsp.	sugar
1 1/2 tsp.	salt
3 1/2 cups	all-purpose flour

CHIVE FILLING:

1 cup	(8 oz.) sour cream
1 cup	minced fresh or frozen chives
1	egg yolk
	butter or margarine, melted

In a bowl, dissolve yeast in water. In a saucepan, heat milk, oil and potatoes to 110 degrees to 115 degrees. Transfer to a mixing bowl; add yeast mixture, egg, sugar and salt. Add enough flour to make a soft dough. Turn onto a floured surface; knead until smooth and elastic, about 6-8 minutes. Place in a greased bowl; turn once to grease top. Cover and let rise in a warm place until doubled, about one hour.

Turn dough onto a floured surface. Roll into a 15-inch by 10-inch rectangle. In a bowl, combine sour cream, chives and egg yolk. Spread over dough to within 1/2 inch of edges. Roll up jellyroll style, starting with a long side; pinch seam to seal. Cut into 1-inch slices. Place cut side down in a 13-inch by 9-inch by 2-inch baking pan. Cover and let rise until doubled, about one hour. Bake at 350 degrees for 30-35 minutes or until golden brown. Brush with butter. Cool on a wire rack. Refrigerate leftovers.

Yield: 15 rolls ❁

REBECCA KOLLS
Television Personality and Flower Show Guest Speaker

Bruschetta

baguette
chopped tomatoes, meaty variety
    like the Roma or Grape
olive oil
balsamic vinegar
shredded basil
coarsely chopped Greek olives
capers
chopped garlic
crumbled blue cheese

You'll notice that with this recipe, there are no measurements! You just mix and taste as you go, which is a great way to do a recipe.

Start off by chopping the tomatoes, put them in a bowl, and then drizzle some olive oil and balsamic vinegar on top. Just keep in mind: 3 parts oil to 1 part vinegar. Next, add the shredded basil, coarsely chopped Greek olives, capers, and garlic. Finally, add the crumbled blue cheese and then mix well.

Now, when you're ready to serve this, put the tomato mixture in a separate bowl surrounded with cut pieces of baguette bread. That way, the guests can serve themselves, and then the bread won't get soggy. If you want to toast the bread, go ahead and do it. Otherwise, fresh cut bread is lovely as well. Either way, once your guests taste this appetizer, it's one they won't forget! ✿

Bruschetta or brusketta: no matter how you say it, this is a great appetizer that tastes as if it came straight from the garden. It's very easy, and I think it's one you'll like!
– Rebecca

MARY MARGARET ROCHFORD

Director of Shows, The Cincinnati
Horticultural Society

Colcannon

1 lb.	kale or cabbage (450 g)
1 lb.	potatoes (450 g)
2	small leeks or green onion tops
1/4 pint	milk or cream (about 150 ml)
	pinch of mace
	salt and pepper
4 oz.	butter, melted (about 100g)

If using the kale, strip from the stalks or likewise remove the stump of cabbage before cooking in boiling salt water until tender but not overcooked. Drain very well and chop finely. Meanwhile, cook the potatoes and while they are cooking chop the leeks or onion tops and simmer them in milk or cream to cover for about 7 minutes. Drain the potatoes, season and mash them well, then stir in the cooked leeks and milk, adding a little more milk if needed.

Finally, blend in the finely chopped kale or cabbage (modern cooks will find a blender or food processor ideal for this.) Add the mace and taste for seasoning. Heat the entire mixture gently, then pile into a warmed dish. Make a small well in the centre and pour in the melted butter.

Recipe from Theodora Fitz Gibbon's "Irish Traditional Food."

Serves 6 🍀

*This is traditionally eaten in Ireland at Hallowe'en or All Hallows'
Day, October 31st. Colcannon at Hallowe'en used to contain a plain
gold ring, a sixpence, a thimble or button; the ring meant marriage within
the year for the person who found it, the sixpence meant wealth, the
thimble spinsterhood and the button bachelorhood.*

▲ Mary Margaret with husband, Fred and Daughter, Maeve.

My Tip on Gardening
Plant what you like where you
like it, and if it doesn't work, move
it. Some plants are like people,
they like moving to a new home.
~ MM

RITA NADER HEIKENFELD

Culinary Expert

Rita's Health Bread

3 cups   self rising flour
1 tsp. ea: dill, fennel, flax, poppy seeds
1   bottle or can, 12 oz., room temperature beer
1 tbsp.   honey
2 tbsp.   unsalted butter, melted or butter spray

Preheat oven to 350. Blend flour and seeds.
Pour in beer and honey. Stir quickly.
Don't overmix. Pour into greased or
sprayed 9x5 pan. Pour butter over.
Bake 40-45 minutes. ❧

DIANNE DUNKELMAN

Speaking of Women's Health, Community Volunteer

Gougères

5 tbsp.	butter
1 tsp.	salt
1/4 tsp.	freshly ground black pepper
1/4 tsp.	freshly ground nutmeg
1 cup	all-purpose flour
1 cup	grated gruyere cheese
5	large eggs, at room temperature (very important)

Preheat oven to 425 degrees.

Add butter, salt, pepper, and nutmeg to one cup of water in medium saucepan and bring to a boil over medium-high heat. When butter melts, reduce heat to low.

Great accompaniment to first course, or, split open and fill with chicken salad, tuna salad, etc.
— Dianne

Add flour to butter-water mixture all at once and cook over low heat, beating with a wooden spoon, for one minute, until mixture pulls away from sides of pan. Remove pan from heat.

Add cheese to pan and beat in with a wooden spoon until well incorporated. Add four of the eggs, one at a time, beating each egg into the batter until thoroughly absorbed. Continue beating mixture until it is smooth, shiny and firm.

Drop batter in small spoonfuls onto a lightly greased cookie sheet to form Gougères. Beat remaining egg with 1/2 tablespoon water, then brush tops of uncooked Gougères with egg wash.

Bake in upper third of oven for 15-20 minutes or until Gougères are golden and doubled in size. Remove from oven and serve hot, or allow to cool to room temperature.

Makes about 3 dozen Gougères. ❋

PAT DEWINE
Cincinnati City Counsil

Pat DeWine's Favorite Rolls

2 pkg.	yeast
1/2 cup	warm water
1 1/2 cup	scalded milk
1/2 cup	margarine or butter
1/2 cup	honey
2	eggs
1 tsp.	salt
6-7 cups	flour

Dissolve yeast in warm water. Mix milk, margarine, honey, eggs and salt and add to yeast mixture. Mix in enough flour to make dough easy to handle. Knead on lightly floured surface 3 to 4 minutes. Place in buttered bowl. Let rise until double (1 1/2 - 2 hours). Punch down. Divide into 4.

Roll each ball into 12" circle. Spread with softened butter. Cut into 12 pie-shaped pieces. Roll up from large end and shape into crescent. Put on baking sheet* and let rise 30 minutes. Bake 15-20 minutes at 350 degree.

At this point, before last rising, you can put them in freezer. Take them out and let them thaw, rise 3 hours before baking. ❧

▲ MICHAEL AND MATTHEW DEWINE

POTS OF FUN

Take one very large flower pot. Find a community sponsor. Enlist an artist to decorate the pot. Plant the pot with a lush array of botanicals. Multiply the effort by 130. Distribute the pots in downtown Cincinnati, Over-the-Rhine, Hyde Park Square and in Covington and Newport, Kentucky. Make sure the pots are watered every day.

The result: Flower Power, a Summer 2002 public art project from the Cincinnati Horticultural Society in partnership with ArtWorks, an art-based employment and job-training program for Greater Cincinnati student artists. Together, the groups and their patrons and volunteers beautified sidewalks and brought smiles and even a few chuckles for summer pedestrians from mid-May through Labor Day.

"It's all part of an effort to pull the community together," Mary Margaret Rochford, president of the Cincinnati Horticultural Society, said at the time. "The beauty of the flowers and the pots will make people in the downtown happy. It will be a legacy. People will see this and think they can do it on their own at their homes."

Generous sponsors anted up the fees ($2,000-$10,000 depending on pot placement), and selected winning designs submitted by local and regional artists. The pots were then decorated in an array of colors and themes, many based on "punny" titles such as "Pot Porri," "We Dig Downtown" or "The Age of Asparagus."

Next the Horticultural Society, with the aid of the Cincinnati Flower Growers Association, stepped in to plant the whimsical pots lushly with flowers and greenery.

After doing their duty scattered about the city, the pots that inspired this *Hotpots* cookbook were brought together again for en masse viewing at the Society's October of 2002 Flower and Farm Fest at Coney Island.

CHS Chairman Marsha Haberer says *Hotpots* came about following the Farm Fest when a recipe book of salads was given at the event's Hoedown. "The recipes were such a hit and we had received so many inquiries about producing a book showcasing the Flower Power Pots, we decided it was a great idea to incorporate the two together."

At the close of the project, Pots not retained by sponsors were sold, with the pro-ceeds used to support future community beautification and horticultural projects. Some live-on, brightening lives at the Battered Women's Shelter, Women Helping Women and the Oakley Senior Center,

Flower Power was a part of Cincinnati Blooms 2002, a program presented by the Cincinnati Horticultural Society. Other components of Cincinnati Blooms included planting flower boxes to brighten the windowsills of Over-the-Rhine, oversized planters dotting Over-the-Rhine street corners and vacant lots and unity gardens in Washington Park planted with the help of hundreds of third graders.

Waving Flags ▶
SPONSOR: FIFTH THIRD BANK,
ARTIST: AMY TANGVALD

To analyze the charms of flowers is like dissecting music; it is one of those things which it is far better to enjoy, than to attempt to fully understand.

— HENRY T. TUCKERMAN

City of the Flying Pinks ▶

SPONSOR: THE OTTO M. BUDIG FAMILY FOUNDATION, ARTIST: JANE SERRIANNE

SWEETS

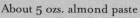

RHODA BROOKS
1997 Flower Show Gala Co-Chair

Raspberry Almond Muffins

About 5 ozs. almond paste
1 stick (1/2) cup butter at room
temperature
3/4 cup granulated sugar
2 large eggs
1 tsp. baking powder
1/2 tsp. baking soda
1 tsp. almond extract
2 cups all purpose flour
1 cup plain yogurt
or buttermilk
About 1/4 cup raspberry preserves

These are a favorite at our house either for a special breakfast or with tea for an afternoon treat.

Heat oven to 350 degrees. Line muffin pans with foil baking cups or spray with cooking spray.

Cut almond paste into 16 pieces and flatten into disks about one inch across. In a large bowl, beat butter until creamy. Beat in sugar until pale and fluffy. Beat in eggs, one at a time, then mix in baking powder, baking soda and almond extract. With rubber spatula, fold in one cup of the flour, then the yogurt and lastly the remaining flour until well blended.

Fill each muffin cup about 1/2 full with batter. Top with a level teaspoon of raspberry preserves, then with a piece of almond paste. Top each muffin with more batter, filling each equally.

Bake 25 to 30 minutes, or until lightly browned. Turn out onto a rack and cool at least 10 minutes. Delicious served warm, but also good at room temperature.

[MY GARDENING TIP]
Grow herbs in large pots in a sunny spot near your kitchen door so you can cut them easily to use fresh from the 'garden'. Chives and tarragon are especially hardy. Mine survive the winter with no protection.

Makes 16 muffins. ❀

LIZ BETEMPS
CHS Board Member

Grandma Hines' Waffles

1 3/4 cups	all purpose flour
2 tsp.	double acting baking powder
1 tbsp.	sugar
3	egg yolks
5 tbsp.	vegetable oil
1 1/2 cups	milk
1 tsp.	vanilla

Sift dry ingredients together in a large mixing
bowl. Mix oil, eggs, and milk into a measuring
cup or small bowl. Fold into the flour mixture.
Pour into hot waffle iron. Yum! ❀

*These hot and delicious waffles are
always served on Sunday mornings, at
the Betemps Farm, "Horse Feathers",
in Clermont County. The recipe is from
my Grandma Hines, a woman who loved
downtown Cincinnati.*

Children in Bloom
SPONSOR: CINCINNATI FLOWER
SHOW, ARTIST: SARAH SMITH
AND CLAIRE KEYS

Hooray for Hollywood
SPONSOR: MARIEMONT HIGH
SCHOOL, ARTIST: MARIEMONT
HIGH SCHOOL STUDENTS

Urnie
SPONSOR: YORK STREET
CAFÉ, ARTIST: B. B. HALL

SWEETS

175

NADINE BRUNNER
Volunteer and small business owner

Banana Nut Bread

This recipe is best cooked a day ahead.

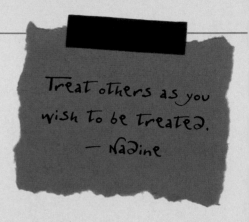

> Treat others as you wish to be treated.
> — Nadine

2 cups	all-purpose flour
1/2 tsp.	salt
1 tsp.	baking soda
1	stick butter
1 cup	sugar
2	eggs, beaten
1 cup	(3 medium) mashed bananas
1/2 cup	sour milk or buttermilk
3/4 cup	walnuts, chopped coarsely
1/2 tsp.	grated lemon peel

Preheat oven to 350 degrees. In medium bowl, sift together first three ingredients. In large bowl, cream butter and sugar; add eggs. Mix in dry ingredients alternately with mashed bananas and sour milk. Add nuts and lemon peel. Pour into a greased and floured 9 x 5 inch loaf pan. Bake for 70 minutes on rack below center of oven. Bake until tester inserted in center comes out clean.

Yields one loaf. *From Tea Time at the Inn, Country Inn Cookbook, 1990.* ❃

◀ **Place to Put Down Roots**
SPONSOR: POTTER HILL HOMES,
ARTIST: TOM POST

Lee LEE CAIN
Former Horticultural Columnist,
The Cincinnati Enquirer

Anzac Biscuits

4 oz.	butter
1 tbsp.	golden syrup
2 tbsp.	boiling water
1 cup	rolled oats
1 1/2 tsp.	bicarbonate soda
3/4 cup	desiccated coconut
1 cup	plain flour
1 cup	sugar

Melt butter and syrup over low heat. Add boiling water mixed with bicarbonate soda. Pour into mixed dry ingredients and mix well. Drop teaspoons of mixture onto greased baking trays leaving room for spreading. Bake in a preheated slow oven at 300 degrees for 20 minutes. Cool on trays for a few minutes, then remove to wire racks. Store in air tight containers. Delicious!

Makes approximately 48 biscuits. ❊

Plant native trees as they are our guarantee of a healthful, beautiful environment.

Anzac biscuits are an Australian favorite, made popular during World War I when there were egg shortages. Sent in food parcels to the troops who became famous as Anzacs (Australia, New Zealand Army Corps).

Kit's Kolassal Kookies

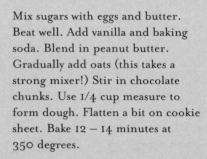

1 1/2	cups brown sugar (packed)
1 1/2	cups granulated sugar
4	eggs
1/2	cup butter (one cube)
1 tsp.	vanilla
2 1/2 tsp.	baking soda
1 jar	18 oz. chunky peanut butter
18 oz.	quick cook oats
1 bag	10 oz. chocolate chunks

Mix sugars with eggs and butter. Beat well. Add vanilla and baking soda. Blend in peanut butter. Gradually add oats (this takes a strong mixer!) Stir in chocolate chunks. Use 1/4 cup measure to form dough. Flatten a bit on cookie sheet. Bake 12 – 14 minutes at 350 degrees.

Makes 2 1/2 to 3 dozen cookies. ❋

My daughter, Maddy, loves making these cookies as much as she loves eating them. (Me too!) Enjoy!

— Kit

ALISON ZIMMERMAN
CHS Board Member

Lemon Cake-Pie

1	lemon
2	eggs, separated
1/4 tsp.	salt
1 cup	milk
1 cup	sugar
2 tbsp.	flour
1 tbsp.	butter

Add the grated rind and juice of 1 lemon to 2 egg yolks. Stir in 1/4 teaspoon salt, 1 cup milk, and 1 cup sugar with 2 tablespoons flour mixed in it. Add 1 tablespoon melted butter. Fold in 2 stiffly beaten egg whites.

Pour into a deep unbaked pie shell and bake until firm, using a 450 degree oven for the first ten minutes, reducing the temperature to 325 degrees for the last 20 minutes. Cool completely.

▲ MARSHA HABERER, DAVID REID AND ALISON ZIMMERMAN

The top of this pie is like a sponge cake and the bottom is like a custard.

Serves 8-10 ❀

"Flowers leave some of their fragrance in the hand that bestows them."
— Chinese proverb

Fancies for the Fairies and other wee mortals!

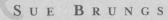

Prepare your favorite cake mix but instead of using a traditional cake pan use a mini cup cake pan. Adjust the baking time to suit the size. There are many decorative paper liners available at craft, hobby or specialty food stores.

When your wee morsels have cooled, the fun begins. Go to your garden and select tiny, new buds or flowers. Be sure to use only plants you know are edible and pesticide free. Wild violets and Johnny Jump-Ups are my favorites.

[On Gardening]

Share your garden. Plants grow best in the company of friends.

PREPARE A SIMPLE FROSTING AS FOLLOWS:

   1 stick   butter at room temperature
1/2 - 3/4 lb. powdered sugar
   3/4 tsp.   vanilla
Little milk or cream

[On Flower Power]

The beauty of flowers colors our lives with hope.

Mix butter and sugar together, add vanilla and cream to give frosting good texture. After each cake is frosted gently place a flower on top of the frosting and press down lightly.

Sprinkle with Fairy Dust (also known as crystal sugar). The icing may be lightly tinted with food coloring to complement your flowers.

As a special treat for your young friends invite them to a tea party. Use a pretty table cloth, real china and your best silver. Make a simple centerpiece of fresh flowers: serve mint tea and your fancy cakes. You may be surprised how much fun a tea party can be. You may also find your older friends are just a wee bit jealous. ❀

Wishing you Fairy Magic
in all you do!
— Sue

A FEW OF MY FAVORITE EDIBLE FLOWERS:

Bee Balm — Monarda	Begonia
Borage	Clove Pink
Chamomile	Lavender
Lemon Balm	Nasturtium
Pineapple Sage ❀	

Look for the best in everyone
you meet. Forgive their
imperfections.
— Sue

Incredible Hot Fudge Sauce

SWEETS

9 tbsp.	cocoa
1 1/2 cups	granulated sugar
dash	salt
1/2 tsp.	cream of tartar
1	12 oz. can evaporated milk
1 tsp.	vanilla
1 tbsp.	butter

Mix together the first four ingredients, then add evaporated milk. Stirring constantly, slowly bring to a boil. Stir for at least one minute in a rolling boil (stirring longer makes the sauce thicker – you can do this to taste).

Remove from heat and add vanilla and butter.

Recipe from the kitchen of Chris Neyer. ❊

▲ BETSY WITH MOM, CHRIS

Serve on your favorite ice cream, cakes, fruit – anything tastes better covered in chocolate!

182

S U S A N   Y O U N G

Freelance Graphic Designer and Friend of CHS

Black and White Cheesecake

🔺 SUSAN WITH SON, JACK

CRUST:

6 tbsp.	butter, room temperature
I/2 cup	sugar
3/4 tsp.	vanilla extract
I/8 tsp.	salt
I/3 cup	unsweetened cocoa powder
3/4 cup	flour

FILLING:

2 I/2 oz.	semisweet or bittersweet chocolate
I/4 cup	water
3	pkg. cream cheese (8 oz.)
I I/4 cups	sugar
I/2 tsp.	vanilla extract
2	large eggs

*Garnish with chocolate
curls and serve with
fresh raspberry sauce.
Delicious!
– Susan*

Preheat oven to 350 degrees.

Beat butter, sugar, vanilla and salt until smooth. Blend in cocoa. Mix in flour until barely incorporated, still crumbly. Firmly pat into bottom of 9" springform pan. Bake for I5 minutes and remove from oven. Reduce oven temperature to 325 degrees.

For filling, melt chocolate with water over low heat until smooth. Beat cream cheese in large bowl. Add sugar gradually until smooth. Add vanilla and eggs beating just until mixed. Set aside I cup of batter. Pour remainder into crust.

Stir warm chocolate into reserved batter. Pour a thick ring into pan and use a knife to marbleize.

Bake I hour and I0 minutes or until fork comes out clean. Chill 4 hours. ❊

PETER AND TINA FRAMPTON
Musician and 2001 Flower Show Honorary Guests

Pumpkin–Cheese Roll

3	eggs
1 cup	sugar
1 tsp.	lemon juice
1 tsp.	ginger
1/2 tsp.	nutmeg
1/4 tsp.	salt
1 tsp.	soda
3/4 cup	flour
2/3 cup	pumpkin
1 cup	nuts, chopped

FILLING:

1 cup	powdered sugar
1	8 ounce package cream cheese, softened
1 tsp.	vanilla
4 tbsp.	butter or margarine

Beat eggs on high speed for 1 minute. Gradually add sugar, lemon juice, spices, salt and soda. Fold in flour and pumpkin. Blend in chopped nuts. Spread in a greased and floured jelly roll pan (or cookie sheet). Sprinkle nuts on top.

Bake at 375 degrees for 20 minutes. Turn out on a towel sprinkled with powdered sugar. Roll like a jelly roll and set aside. Combine filling ingredients.

When cake is cool, unroll and spread with filling. Roll back up like a jelly roll.

Makes twelve servings. 🌼

JIM ANDERSON
President and C.E.O.
Cincinnati Children's Hospital Medical Center

Butterscotch Brownies

1/2 lb.   butter
1 box   light brown sugar
4   eggs
2 cups   flour
1/2 tsp.   baking powder
1 tsp.   vanilla
2 cups   chopped nuts

MIXTURE:

1 cup   light brown sugar
2 tbsp.   milk
2 tbsp.   butter
1 tbsp.   flour
   pinch of salt
1/4 tsp.   vanilla

Melt butter, add sugar and unbeaten eggs one at a time. Mix well. Add sifted flour to which the baking powder has been added, then add the vanilla and nuts. Pour into a well greased oblong cake pan and bake at 350 degrees for about 40 minutes. Combine all ingredients for the mixture in a saucepan and mix well. Bring to a boil and let boil for 1 minute. Pour over hot cake.

Makes 24 squares. 🌸

▲ JIM WITH MARY MARGARET ROCHFORD AND MARSHA HABERER

RON WISE
Owner and Chef, Rondo's

Almond Krokant with Glazed Bananas & Vanilla Ice Cream

KROKANT — ALMOND BRITTLE

2 cups	sugar
1/4 lemon	juice only
11 oz.	toasted almond slices

Place sugar & lemon juice in heavy bottom saucepan. Cook on medium heat until "hard crack" stage. Remove from heat, add almonds & pour onto a buttered marble slab. Let cool & roughly chop in cuisinart.

GLAZED BANANAS:

4	bananas — peeled & cut in 1/2 lengthwise
1 tbsp.	butter
1/4 cup	sugar in the raw dash of favorite rum

Sauté bananas in butter, add sugar & deglaze with rum. Sprinkle krokant on the plate, scoop ice cream onto the middle of the plate, and arrange the bananas over the top of the ice cream.

Yields 8 Portions ✻

▲
Watching Your Urnings Grow
SPONSOR: BARTLETT & CO.,
ARTIST: JENNIFER SIERRA

judy **JUDY GIBBONS**
Community Volunteer

Heavenly Torte

TORTE:

6 egg whites,
room temperature
1/4 tsp. salt
1/2 tsp. cream of tartar
1 tsp. vanilla
1 1/2 cups sugar

TOPPING:

8 oz. whipping cream
whipped
Strawberries, sliced

Preheat oven to 450 degrees.

Beat egg whites, salt, cream of tartar
and vanilla until frothy. Gradually add
sugar, small amounts at a time, beating
until stiff peaks are formed and the
sugar is dissolved. Butter the bottom of
a spring form pan and pour mixture
into it. Place pan on the center rack in
450 degree oven and turn oven off.
Let dry in oven (do not open door)
for at least three hours.

Remove torte from pan and spread
whipped cream over it. Refrigerate
immediately. Before serving, cover
top with strawberries.

Serves 8 ✳

*The discovery of a new
dish does more for human
happiness than the discovery
of a new star.
– Anthelme Brillat-Savarin*

HAZEL PARRISH

Broker, Comey & Shepherd Realtors and Flower
Show Volunteer Chairperson

English Trifle

This traditional dessert can be served with afternoon tea
or for a more formal dinner party.

	pound cake or jelly roll
	apricot or raspberry jam
	fruit (either fresh, frozen or canned)
	custard
	sweet sherry
	heavy whipping cream
1 pint	milk
4	egg yolks, beaten
2 tbsp.	sugar
	toasted slivered almonds or
	grated chocolate to decorate

[ON FLOWER POWER EXHIBIT]

*A wonderful idea, yet
another gift to the city. My
favorite is the blue & white
Chinese willow pattern.*

Slice the pound cake, spread with jam and put at the bottom of a glass trifle dish or a dish with straight sides. If using jelly roll, you can omit the jam and place the slices around the sides of the dish as well as at the bottom. Sprinkle with Sherry. Add a layer of fruit, your choice. I like to use mandarin oranges and frozen raspberries. Make another layer of pound cake, Sherry and fruit.

Heat the milk with the sugar until the sugar has dissolved. Pour the milk over the egg yolks, beating all the time.

Return to the saucepan, and stir over a moderate heat until the liquid will coat the back of a spoon. Do not allow the custard to boil or it will curdle.

Remove from the heat and stir to prevent a skin forming. Allow to cool, covered.

Pour the cold custard over the pound cake and fruit.

About 30 minutes before serving, cover the top with the whipped cream piled high, and decorate with nuts or chocolate or glace fruits. ❧

Gardening Tip –
Keep the picture labels from your new
plants in a plastic 4 x 6 album.
They are easy to refer to for names and
growing information.

Montessori at The New School - Where Knowledge Flowers
SPONSOR: THE NEW SCHOOL,
ARTIST: NEW SCHOOL STUDENTS

Hog Wild Flowers
SPONSOR: HELEN WILLIAMS,
ARTIST: CINDY HACKNEY

Sea Garden
SPONSOR: NEWPORT
AQUARIUM, ARTIST:
SUSAN WECHSLER

SWEETS

189

JOAN CROWE
Community Volunteer

Apricot Almond Bars

SWEETS

1 cup   butter
1/2 cup   sugar
1/2 tsp. vanilla
2 cups   sifted flour
1   15 oz. jar apricot jam
2   egg whites
1/2 tsp. almond extract
1 cup   powdered sugar
1/4 cup   slivered almonds.

Cream butter, sugar and vanilla until light and fluffy. Add flour and mix thoroughly. Spread in a 13x9x2 pan and bake at 350 degrees for 15 minutes. Cool. Spread apricot jam over crust gently. Beat egg whites and almond extract using electric beater. Beat in sugar gradually. Mixture is thin and acts as a glaze. Spread over jam carefully and top with almonds. Bake at 400 degrees for 20 minutes or until delicately browned. Cut while still warm.

Serves 10 -12 ✳

◀ **Red, White & Blooming**
SPONSOR: TIFFANY & CO.,
ARTIST: JOANN HEURICH

Kirk's Favorite Dessert — Chocolate Crème

6 oz.	chocolate bits
4 tbsp.	cold water
5	eggs separated
1 tsp.	vanilla
	freshly whipped cream

A balanced diet is a chocolate chip cookie in each hand. —Marie

Melt chocolate bits and water in pan over low heat until well blended. Remove from heat and stir in egg yolks, which have been well beaten. Fold in stiffly beaten egg whites and continue to stir until all is well blended.

Pour into individual serving containers. Refrigerate at least 5 hours or preferably overnight. Serve with a bit of whipped cream. Add small sprig of mint and grated chocolate swirls to top of whipped cream.

For real chocolate lovers, use a champagne glass. For those calorie counters, use a demitasse cup.

Serves 4-6 depending on size of container. ❋

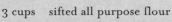

WILLIE CARDEN
Director of the Cincinnati Park Board

Lemon Pound Cake

3 cups	sifted all purpose flour
1/2 tsp.	baking soda
1/2 tsp.	salt
2	sticks of unsalted butter softened (use 1 tablespoon to butter pan)
2 tsp.	vanilla extract
2 tsp.	lemon extract
4	large eggs (at room temperature)
1/2 cup	buttermilk
1/2 cup	sour cream
	10" bundt or tube pan

Whisk together all dry ingredients in a bowl.

In another bowl, cream butter and sugar until fluffy. Add vanilla and lemon extracts. Add one egg yolk at a time, (4 total). In another bowl, mix together buttermilk and sour cream until smooth. Add in flour mixture in thirds alternately with buttermilk mixture.

In another bowl, beat egg whites until stiff peaks form. Fold beaten egg whites into batter. Use 10-inch bundt or tube pan and pour in batter. Bake 50-55 minutes in a 350 degree oven. Cool 15-20 minutes and then take out of pan.

When cool serve with glaze or favorite toppings. ❧

Baked Fruit

Use large size 20-29 ounce cans of fruit.

1	can apricot halves
1	can dark cherries, pitted
1	can sliced peaches
1	can pear halves
1	can chunk pineapple
1 1/2	sticks of butter
4 tsp.	curry power
3/4 cup	light brown sugar

Drain fruit, doing the cherries separately. Cut peaches and pears into smaller sections. Combine all the fruits except the cherries and arrange in a shallow baking dish. Place the cherries on the top layer. Melt the butter and add the curry powder and sugar, blending well. Pour this mixture over the fruit, cover with foil and refrigerate for 8-10 hours. Uncover and bake at 350 degrees for 50-60 minutes.

This mixture can also be baked in a micro-wave oven. If necessary, mandarin oranges and maraschino cherries could be used as substitute fruits.

Serves 8 - 10 ❀

Flower Mania.
SPONSOR CINCINNATIAN HOTEL,
ARTIST: SCOTT JONES

Famous Cats - A Gardening 'Cat'-astrophe
SPONSOR: CINCINNATI FLOWER SHOW, ARTIST: LAURA ALLEN

Pretty as a Peacock
SPONSOR: CINCINNATI ZOO AND BOTANICAL GARDENS, ARTIST: KIRSTEN STAMATES

BREADS & DESSERTS

Chocolate éclairs

PATE À CHOUX (FOR ÉCLAIRS AND CREAM PUFFS)

I	quart water
10 1/2 oz.	butter, cut in pieces
I oz.	sugar
1/2 oz.	salt
I lb. I oz.	sifted bread flour
14	eggs (1 pound 5 oz)

Put water, butter, sugar and salt in a mixer bowl and bring to a boil over stove. Over medium heat, add the flour all at once stirring vigorously for approximately three minutes. With the mixer on low speed, add eggs one at a time to hot flour paste to incorporate; increase speed to make smooth.

Pipe out desired shapes. Egg wash for shiny crust. Bake at 425 degrees for approximately 40 minutes or until dry on the inside.

Cool and fill puffs.

Makes 60 puffs. ❁

Decoupot
SPONSOR: AUGUST A.
RENDIGS JR. FOUNDATION,
ARTIST: JENNIFER REIS

These delicious éclairs are served at the Cincinnati Flower Show Afternoon Teas.

BASIC GANACHE

16 oz.	heavy cream
1 1/2 lb.	semi-sweet chocolate finely chopped

Bring heavy cream to a boil. Remove from heat, add chocolate and stir constantly until melted.

Makes 2 1/2 pounds ✿

PASTRY CREAM

1 quart	milk
4 oz.	sugar
3 oz.	cornstarch
8	eggs (12 oz.)
2 oz.	butter
4 oz.	sugar

Combine milk with first sugar, bring to a boil. Combine second sugar with cornstarch, add eggs and mix until smooth. Temper egg mixture, add to milk, return to boil. Remove from heat, add butter. Pour into a hotel pan, cover and refrigerate.

Makes 3 pounds, 9 oz ✿

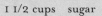

JEANE ELLIOTT
CHS Marketing and Administration Director

Malibu Carrot Cake

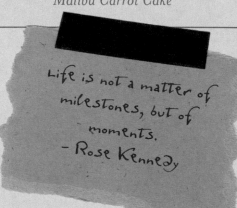

Life is not a matter of milestones, but of moments.
— Rose Kennedy

1 1/2 cups	sugar
3	eggs
1 1/8 cups	vegetable oil
1 1/2 cups	flour
1 1/2 tsp.	baking soda
1 1/2 tsp.	cinnamon
2 1/4 cups	roughly grated carrots
1 1/2 cups	raisins
1 1/2 cups	chopped nuts

Mix sugar, eggs, oil. When smooth, add flour sifted with baking soda. Blend, then add cinnamon, carrots, raisins and nuts.

Amounts of nuts and raisins can be increased to taste.

Bake at 325 degrees for one hour in a well greased 9-inch square pan. Test, as it may need more time as it is a moist cake.

Keeps well in refrigerator.

Ice with a favorite cream cheese icing such as this one:

PHILADELPHIA CREAM CHEESE ICING:
1/2	stick butter (1/4 cup)
4 oz.	cream cheese
	Soften both to room temperature and then add:
1 cup	powdered sugar
1 tsp.	vanilla ❋

Given to me years ago by my California cousin! Delicious.
— Jeane

LAURA PULFER

Author and Enquirer Columnist

Kentucky Derby Pie

1 cup   sugar
1/2 cup   flour
2   eggs, beaten
1/2 cup   butter, melted and cooled
1 cup   chopped pecans
1 cup   semisweet chocolate chips
1 tsp.   vanilla
1   unbaked 9-inch pie shell

Pre-heat oven to 350 degrees.

Mix sugar, flour, eggs and melted butter and beat
well. (I usually do it with a spoon — the mixer gets
too clogged.) Add nuts, chocolate chips and
vanilla, mixing thoroughly. Pour into pie shell.
Bake about 25 minutes — until surface is golden
brown. Let cool before serving. It's sloppy if you
try to serve it warm. ❀

Lettuce Entertain You
SPONSOR: OHIO ASSOCIATION
OF GARDEN CLUBS, REGION 4,
ARTIST: COOKI THIER

Flowers in Your Cup
SPONSOR: CHIP HUNTER OF THE
HHB PARTNERS, INC. REALTORS
AND CHARLIE COOKE SOCCER
SCHOOL, ARTIST: JANET BYRNES
AND JEFFREY VAN SLUYS

*I perhaps owe
having become a
painter to flowers.
— Claude Monet*

Jungle Lacy's
SPONSOR: PAMELA B.
ROSENBAUM, ARTIST:
NOELLE WEDIG

SUSAN KAHN
1994 Flower Show Gala Co-Chair

Apricot Nectar Cake

This is a family favorite!

    1   box yellow cake
    4   eggs
 1/2 cup sugar
 1/2 cup Wesson oil
   1 cup apricot nectar glaze

Mix 4 minutes.

Bake at 350 degrees for 50 minutes in bundt cake pan.

GLAZE:

    1 cup   sugar
 1/2 cup   buttermilk
 1/2 tsp.   soda
 1/2 tsp.   vanilla
 1/2 cup   margarine

Combine ingredients and boil 1-5 minutes while stirring constantly.

Make slashes in cake and pour glaze over
cake. ❀

▲ *I Can't Ever Leaf Cincinnati!*
SPONSOR: GREATER CINCINNATI CHAMBER
OF COMMERCE, ARTIST: BEV KIRK

CHAREE MADDUX
Owner, with husband Bob, Delhi Garden
Centers and Flower Show Exhibitor

Charee's Banana Nut Bread

1/2 cup	butter
1 1/2 cups	sugar
3	eggs
1 1/2 cups	sour cream
2 tsp.	soda
1 tsp.	vanilla
2 1/2	bananas
1/2 tsp.	salt
2 1/2 cups	flour
1 cup	chopped pecans

Cream together butter, sugar and eggs. Mix sour cream and soda together in separate bowl and let stand until foamy. Add rest of ingredients to the above mixtures and mix well. Place into 2 greased and floured 9 x 5 bread pans and bake 50 minutes at 350 degrees until toothpick comes out clean.

Note: Use very ripe bananas. It is also okay to use egg beaters and low-fat sour cream and margarine. ✳

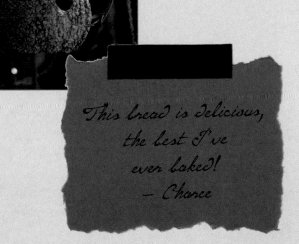

This bread is delicious, the best I've ever baked!
— Charee

JOHN ANGELO
Flower Show Consultant/Advisor

Key Lime Pie

S W E E T S

CRUST:

2	2 oz. squares unsweetened chocolate
1/4 cup	butter
1 1/2 cups	graham cracker crumbs
1/4 cup	sugar

FILLING:

1	can sweetened condensed milk (14 oz.)
3	egg yolks
2/3 cup	Key lime juice (lemon or regular lime juice can be substituted, but then it isn't truly a Key lime pie)
3	egg whites

Melt chocolate in a double boiler or in a microwave on low heat, add butter to melt, mix with graham cracker crumbs and sugar and press into 9" pie pan. Cool.

Beat egg yolks, add sweetened condensed milk and Key lime juice. Set aside while you whip egg whites into stiff peaks, then fold the egg whites into the filling batter and scoop into the pie pan.

Bake for 10 minutes at 250 degrees. When cool, top with lightly sweetened whipped cream. Garnish with chocolate curls or shavings.

This is a recipe favorite from 1995 made by "The Chafer Caterer". ✿

Lavender Cookies

5/8 cup	butter
1/2 cup	sugar
1 tbsp.	dried lavender flowers
1	egg beaten
1 1/2 cups	self-rising flour (cake flour)
	assorted leaves and flowers
	to decorate

Preheat oven to 350 degrees. Cream butter and sugar, stir in egg. Mix in crushed flowers and flour. Drop by spoonfuls on greased cookie sheet. Bake 15 to 20 minutes or until golden brown. Decorate immediately. 🌸

BOBBIE STERNE
Former Mayor, City of Cincinnati

Apple Pudding

SWEETS

6 or 7	apples
3/4 cups	sugar
1/2 cup	butter
1 cup	sugar
1	egg, beaten
1 cup	cake flour
2 tsp.	vanilla
1 tsp.	baking powder

Pare and slice apples. Mix sugar into apples and place in greased baking dish.

Mix butter, sugar, egg, flour, vanilla and baking powder for batter. Pour over apple mix and bake 45 minutes at 350 degrees.

Serve with sweetened whipped cream. ❀

Gardens are not created or made, they unfold, spiraling open
like the silk petals of an evening primrose flower
to reveal the ground plot of the mind
and heart of the gardener and the good earth.
– Wendy Johnson

roSiP **ROSIE ALLEN**

Flower & Farm Fest Volunteer

Almond–Orange Biscotti

2 1/4 cups all-purpose flour
1 1/4 cups sugar
  1/4 tsp. baking powder
            pinch of salt
       3   eggs, lightly beaten
  1 tbsp.   vegetable oil
  1/4 tsp. almond extract
            finely grated zest of
            1 orange
  3/4 cup   coarsely chopped
            almonds

Mix flour, sugar, baking powder
and salt together in a food processor.
Add remaining ingredients. Pulse
until a dough has been formed. Divide dough in half. Shape dough into
two flat-bottomed cylinders, 1 inch high, 2 1/2 inches wide and 8 inches
long. Pat down top slightly. Bake at 350 degrees for 30-35 minutes,
until lightly colored on top. Remove from oven and cool slightly.
Holding a long sharp serrated knife by the handle and the tip cut cylinders
diagonally into 3/4 inch slices. Carefully place slices back on baking
sheet, cut side down, and return them to the oven for about 15 minutes
more, until sides are golden and biscotti have dried a bit. Remove from
oven and cool on wire racks. This biscotti should be hard and crunchy.

Yield: 20-24 ✿

The focal point of celebrations with family and
friends is the food, but having time to enjoy the
company of others is the reward.

LIZ RAGOUZIS
Flower Show Chairperson and
2001 Volunteer of the Year

Orange Ribbon Chiffon Loaf

1 cup	flour, sifted
3/4 cup	sugar
1 1/2 tsp.	baking powder
1/2 tsp.	salt
1/4 cup	oil
3	unbeaten egg yolks
1/4 cup	
+ 2 tbsp.	cold water or orange juice (I always use orange juice)
1 1/2 tbsp.	grated orange rind
1/2 cup	egg whites (about 4)
1/4 tsp.	cream of tartar

Heat oven to 325 degrees. Sift first 4 ingredients into a bowl. Make a well, add oil, egg yolks, liquid and rind. Beat with spoon until smooth or with electric mixer, medium speed, one minute.

Measure egg whites, cream of tartar into large bowl. Beat by hand until whites form very stiff peaks or with electric mixer, high speed, 3 to 5 minutes. DO NOT UNDERBEAT. Pour egg yolk mixture gradually over beaten whites, folding just until blended. Pour into ungreased loaf pan, 9 x 5 x 2 1/2.

Bake 50 to 55 minutes, or until top springs back when lightly touched. Turn pan upside down with edges on two other pans. Hang until cold. To remove, loosen sides with spatula, turn pan over, hit edge sharply on table. Cut cake into 3 even layers. Spread with your favorite thick orange filling and whipped cream. Chill 1 to 2 hours. Makes 8 to 10 slices, 1 inch thick. ❧

Daffodils are separated into 13 Divisions—
according to their appearance.
Narcissus are daffodils and daffodils are narcissus
Jonquils are daffodils and/or narcissus, but
specifically fall into Division 7 (jonquilla).
Deer will not eat daffodils.

CLEAR ORANGE FILLING:

1 cup	sugar
4 tbsp.	cornstarch
1/2 tsp.	salt
1 cup	orange juice
2 tbsp.	grated orange rind
1 1/2 tbsp.	lemon juice
2 tbsp.	butter

Mix filling ingredients in sauce pan.
Bring to rolling boil and boil one
minute, stirring constantly. Chill
before using. Whip one pint whipping
cream, lightly sweeten. Spread each
layer with orange filling, then cream.
Stack layers and then cover whole cake
with whipped cream. Cake may be
decorated with thin orange slices or
toasted almonds. ❋

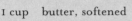

JOE HALE - President, Cinergy Foundation
LINDA HALE - 1997 Flower Show Gala Co-Chair

Fresh Raspberry Butter Cake

SWEETS

1 cup	butter, softened
1 cup + 2 tbsp.	sugar
4	eggs
1 1/2 tsp.	vanilla
1 1/2 tsp.	baking powder
1 2/3 cup	flour, sifted
1 1/2 cup	fresh red raspberries
1 tbsp.	sugar
2 tsp.	cornstarch
2 tsp.	lemon zest

GARNISH:
Rothschild Gourmet Red
            Raspberry Sauce
Fresh red raspberries

Preheat oven to 350 degrees. Add butter and sugar to the bowl of an electric mixer. Beat just to combine. Add eggs one at a time to incorporate. Add the vanilla and continue beating for 1-2 minutes. Turn mixer down to low and add the flour and baking powder gradually. Mix only to incorporate.

Mix together remaining sugar and cornstarch. Add raspberries and lemon zest and combine.

Add one half of the batter to a greased 9" spring form pan. Carefully spoon the raspberries over the cake batter. Add the remaining batter over the raspberries and smooth the top. Bake for 40-45 minutes or until cake is springy in the middle. Cool slightly.

To serve — place a small amount of raspberry sauce on a dessert plate. Top with a slice of cake and toss a few fresh raspberries around the cake.

One of the 'Afternoon Dessert Delicacies' from the 1999 Flower and Farm Fest. ❀

Bran Fruit Loaf

This is very old (30 years or so) recipe from the outside of a Kellogg's cornflakes packet— brilliant, cheap and never goes wrong!

4 oz.	All-Bran	(125g)
5 oz.	sugar	(150g)
10 oz.	mixed fruit	(275g)
1/2 pint	milk	(125 mls)
4 oz.	self raising flour	(125g)

[MY COOKING TIP]

Peel potatoes and prepare vegetables before going out gardening - because you invariably forget about time and come in too late.
– Helen

Put All-Bran, sugar and dried fruit in a basin and mix them well together. Stir in milk and leave to stand for 1/2 hour. Sieve in the flour, mixing well, and pour mixture into a well-greased 2 lb. loaf tin. Bake in a moderate oven (Gas No. 4) for about 1 1/4 hours. Turn out of tin and allow to cool. Cut into slices and spread with butter. Keeps for ages! ✳

Never pass a weed.
– Helen

JAY KORTE
Friend of the Flower Show and Owner of Flower Framers

Chocolate Toffee Torte

CRUST:

10 oz.	pecan halves and pieces
1/2 cup	sugar
1/2 cup	unsalted butter, melted

CHOCOLATE LAYER:

1/2 lb.	semisweet chocolate
1 cup	heavy cream
2 tbsp.	light corn syrup

TOFFEE LAYER:

4	extra large eggs
1 cup	unsalted butter
2 oz.	unsweetened chocolate
1 1/2 cups	light brown sugar
2 tsp.	very strong coffee or espresso

MOCHA TOPPING:

1 1/2 cups	heavy cream
3/4 cup	powdered sugar
1 tsp.	vanilla
1 tsp.	coffee essence, or coffee liqueur (Kahlua), or strong coffee

GARNISH:

Chocolate shavings and chocolate mocha beans (optional)

CRUST:

Coarsely chop pecans in food processor, using the on and off method. Combine the pecans, sugar and butter. Press into bottom of a greased 9-inch springform pan. Freeze crust for 30 minutes. Preheat oven to 350 degrees. Bake crust about 10-15 minutes, until lightly brown. Cool.

CHOCOLATE LAYER:

Combine semisweet chocolate and cream in heavy saucepan. Cook over medium heat until chocolate is melted, stirring frequently. Add corn syrup. Pour mixture over crust. Chill until set, about 1-2 hours or overnight.

As long as nature guides your gardening, you will never be dissatisfied with the results. Study nature for hours, days, weeks, and years. Not a moment will be wasted and you will never graduate.

– Jay

TOFFEE LAYER:

Bring eggs and butter to room temperature. In a double boiler, melt unsweetened chocolate. Using an electric mixer, beat the eggs. Gradually add brown sugar and beat well. Add melted chocolate and beat well. Add softened butter, one tablespoon at a time, and continue beating until the mixture is thoroughly combined. (Don't worry if the mixture looks separated. Keep beating and it will come together.) Add coffee or espresso. Spread toffee mixture over the chocolate layer and chill until set, about 3 hours or overnight.

MOCHA TOPPING:

Combine cream, powdered sugar, vanilla, and coffee essence; beat until stiff.

Run knife around edge of cake; remove sides of springform pan. Spread mocha topping over top of cake. Garnish with chocolate shavings and chocolate mocha beans, if desired.

MARY MARGARET ROCHFORD
Director of Shows, The Cincinnati Horticultural Society

Poppy Seed Bread

2 oz.	poppies
1 cup	buttermilk
1 cup	butter/margarine
2 cups	sugar (save 1/2 cup)
4	eggs
2 1/2 cups	flour
1 1/2 tsp.	baking powder
1/2 tsp.	baking soda
1 tsp.	almond extract
1 tsp.	cinnamon

Soak poppy seed in buttermilk 10-15 minutes.

Cream butter & 1 1/2 cups sugar. Beat eggs in one at a time. Sift flour, baking powder, and baking soda. Add to creamed mixture. Add alternate flour & poppy seed in buttermilk mixture. Blend in the almond extract. In a separate bowl, mix 1/2 cup of sugar with teaspoon of cinnamon. Spoon batter into greased 10" tube pan. Shake cinnamon & sugar mixture alternatively and sprinkle remaining mixture on top.

Bake in oven for 50 minutes to an hour on 350. Let stand in pan at least 10 minutes. ❁

▲ THE LATE ROSEMARY VEREY AND MARY MARGARET

brunhilde

BRUNHILDE KUNZEL,
Spouse of CSO/CPO Conductor, Maestro Erich Kunzel

Plum Tart (Zwetschken Kuchen)

CRUST:

1 3/4	sticks	unsalted butter
2 1/4	cup	flour
3 1/2	tbsp.	sour cream
3/4	tsp.	salt

Preheat oven to 325 degrees. Butter the bottom and sides of a 9 x 13 inch glass pan. Fit a food processor with steel blade. Cut butter into chunks. Place into bowl with the flour, sour cream and salt. Process until the dough pulls into a ball. Gently pat dough evenly on bottom and sides of prepared pan.

▲ MAESTRO KUNZEL

FILLING:

3 tbsp.	flour
1/2 cup	sour cream
20-24	Italian plums or other plums
2	eggs
1 1/2 cups	sugar

Pit and slice plums into quarters. Cover the crust completely with rows of sliced plums. Beat eggs with the sugar, flour and sour cream until well blended. Pour this mixture carefully over the plums. Bake tart for 45 to 60 minutes or until custard is set. Allow the tart to cool and serve with best quality vanilla ice cream.

Reprinted from "Rhapsody of Recipes" by kind permission of the Friends of the Pops. ❀

FLOWER POWER POTS

◀ *We Dig Downtown*
SPONSOR: U.S. BANK, ARTIST: MARK EBERHARD

Croc Pot

SPONSOR: REUVEN AND CATE KATZ, TIM AND SUE CLARKE AND DANIEL
AND CLAIRE HUGHES, ARTIST: ANN APPLEGATE-KATZ

Croc-Pot
CINCINNATI HORTICULTURAL SOCIETY
FLOWER POWER
CROC POT

Formal Garden
SPONSOR: HYDE PARK SQUARE,
ARTIST: CARRIE LYNN COOKE

ENTREÉS

SANDWICHES, SIDES & SAVORY FARE

SWEETS